Movement studies and physical education

Also edited by J. E. Kane
Psychological Aspects of Physical Education and Sport

Movement studies and physical education

A handbook for teachers

edited by

J. E. Kane
Principal
West London Institute of Higher Education

Routledge & Kegan Paul
London, Henley and Boston

First published in 1977
by Routledge & Kegan Paul Ltd
39 Store Street,
London WC1E 7DD,
Broadway House,
Newtown Road,
Henley-on-Thames,
Oxon RG9 1EN and
9 Park Street,
Boston, Mass. 02108, USA
Photoset in 10 on 12 Times
by Kelly and Wright, Bradford-on-Avon, Wiltshire
and printed in Great Britain by
Lowe & Brydone Ltd

British Library Cataloguing in Publication Data

Movement studies in physical education.
1. Physical education and training—Great Britain.
I. Kane, John Edward
613.7'07'1041 GV443 77–30133

ISBN 0–7100–8775–6
ISBN 0–7100–8684–9 Pbk

Contents

Introduction

J. E. Kane

The Handbook for Teachers of Physical Education and Movement Studies is one of a series sponsored by the University of London Institute of Education as a contribution to understanding and curriculum development in subject areas.

The curriculum area which has direct links with drill, systematised exercise systems and physical training tends to be currently represented within the educational system encapsulated by the schools as physical education. This term, physical education, has had currency for at least thirty years and continues to emphasise the educational relevance of learning experiences in organised and free forms of games, play, dance, sport and general physical activity. The contribution of physical education to the general educative process has been convincingly and successfully agreed and accepted in Britain, so that it is possible now to point to a very substantial national investment and commitment in this area of the school curriculum.

So successful has been the impact of physical education on our educational system that it has given rise in recent years to the identification and development of an elaborated and multi-disciplinary area of rigorous academic study centred on human movement. It may be that this elaborated study area, currently designated Human Movement Studies, was shaped by the forces that precipitated the fundamental re-assessment of courses in colleges of education and led to the introduction of the BEd degree. At any rate, the academic perspectives and opportunities of four-year degree courses in the colleges provided the stimulus and focus for the intensive study of human movement, especially as manifested in skilful and expressive behaviour, which has involved, for example, philosophical speculations, biomechanical analyses and psychological and sociological interpretations. More recently, the increasing number of professional and non-professional undergraduate and graduate courses in this area offered in universities and colleges is a firm indication of the establishment of Movement Studies as a thriving and worthwhile academic discipline.

During the development of this academic emphasis directed towards the analysis and synthesis of human movement, there may have been some initial and related reduction in the general commitment to re-appraisal and renewal in physical education. Understandably, the opening up of a new multi-disciplinary area of study unfettered by vocational ties presented compelling attractions to lecturers and their students if not to school teachers, and physical education began to be interpreted and defined as an applied form of movement knowledge concerned with the organisation of appropriate learning experiences for the educational curriculum. The current assessment must certainly be that, while the intensification of the study of human movement has opened up an intrinsically satisfying academic area, it has also indicated a wider applicability of movement knowledge—within education and outside it—than had previously been suggested.

There is no doubt that there has been in recent years a direct and obvious application of the elaborated study of human movement to the physical education curriculum in schools. There is already a noticeable re-organisation of many curricula to include not only important functional (including sports) skills but also expressive skills. Cognitive and affective elements are also finding a place with the skills in current curricula. Such developments may alternatively be taken to be some indication of a gathering force for curriculum renewal which has been unduly delayed in physical education but is now clearly recognisable.

This Handbook for Teachers is a collection of specially written articles which represent an important contribution to perspectives and meaning in the study of human movement and to the curriculum of physical education for schools with which it is directly linked. The Handbook is divided into five parts.

Part 1 contains papers which, together, attempt to characterise the area of human movement studies and indicate its perspectives.

Part 2 deals with the ways in which movement may be linked

with communication in general and with language in particular.

Part 3 considers the implication of related scientific thought and development for interpretation in movement analysis and physical education.

Part 4, which is appropriately the largest section, is given over to consideration of the physical education curriculum in schools.

Part 5 is a reference section, where teaching materials and sources of information are listed.

The Handbook was planned by an editorial sub-committee of the Institute of Education Movement Studies Committee. The Editor wishes to acknowledge the co-operation of editorial colleagues, the contributors and the Institute's Publication Officer in this enterprise.

List of contributors

J. E. Kane	Principal of the West London Institute of Higher Education, Isleworth, Middlesex.
B. Jagger	Principal Lecturer in Physical Education, Avery Hill College of Education, Eltham, Kent.
R. L. Groves	Principal Lecturer in Physical Education and Movement Studies, West London Institute of Higher Education, Isleworth, Middlesex.
S. E. Archbutt	Principal Lecturer in Movement Studies, Nonington College, Dover, Kent.
M. J. Cooper	Principal Lecturer in Physical Education, Kingston Polytechnic, Kingston-upon-Thames, Surrey.
E. M. Hinks	Formerly Principal of Nonington College of Physical Education, but now retired.
M. North	Director of the Laban Centre for Movement and Dance, Goldsmith's College, New Cross, London.
A. J. Smith	Lecturer in Ergonomics and Mechanics, National College of Agricultural Engineering, Silsoe, Bedfordshire.

List of Contributors

J. G. P. Williams	Medical Director, Farnham Park Rehabilitation Centre, Farnham Park, Farnham Royal, Buckinghamshire.
E. Hoyle	Professor of Education, Bristol University, Bristol.
Dudley F. Cooper	Principal Lecturer in Movement Studies, St Mary's College, Strawberry Hill, Twickenham, Middlesex.
Gordon Underwood	Principal Lecturer in Movement Studies, Nonington College of Physical Education, Dover, Kent.
Irene K. Glaister	Formerly Lecturer in Physical Education, University of Leeds.
Joan W. White	Senior Lecturer in Physical Education, Roehampton Institute of Higher Education, Southlands College, London SW19.
L. Almond	Research Fellow, Department of Physical Education, Loughborough College of Education, Loughborough, Leicestershire.
O. M. Chapman	Head of Department of English and Expressive Arts, Avery Hill College of Education, Eltham, Kent.
H. W. Wilkinson	Principal Lecturer in Physical Education, Roehampton Institute of Higher Education, Southlands College, London SW19.
Alan Gibbon	Inspector of Physical Education, Inner London Education Authority.

Part 1

Movement studies and physical education—perspectives and characterisation

1

A characterisation of physical education and human movement

B. Jagger

Introduction

Physical education has paraded under many names during the last hundred years and has seen strange and diverse developments on the way to its present standing. Even now it is a curiously mixed subject containing not only a welter of activities but also many varied teaching approaches including educational, recreational, competitive, coaching and play organisation. In addition, there have been periods of time when men and women taught quite different aspects of the subject in quite different ways, almost making physical education divisive and that much weaker. However, there is evidence that a happier understanding now exists and there is a growing appreciation of the status and standing of physical education in the school setting, in colleges and universities.

Despite these improvements, there is no time for complacency and important questions still must be asked about the subject, and the correct answers must be provided. A deep searching into physical education is necessary, with all its members whether professional or academic coming to certain basic agreements on such questions as:

1 Is physical education in the school setting of understood and accepted educational value?
2 What is the place of recreation in schools?
3 How do we evaluate the efficiency of the subject?
4 What are the general recommendations on curriculum content and the sequential order of teaching?
5 What is the rating of the different methods of teaching?

Much research has been developed within physical education during the last ten years and the above questions have been touched upon without definite answers being provided. Perhaps it is impossible to give definite answers and if this is so, helpful guidelines at least should be available so that teachers can have the backing of colleges and universities towards the establishment of agreed correct answers to these fundamental questions.

Physical education in the school setting

The present time is one when critical enquiry is being levelled by authority at all subjects in the school curriculum and the continuation of some subjects in their existing form is at stake. The curriculum is overloaded and some pruning is needed. Moreover, in the present financial state of the country a hard look may be directed towards the 'expensive' subjects in the school, amongst which physical education is one. On both these counts we in physical education may be vulnerable, and open to the sort of charge that we would not wish. There are pointers towards change from other centres of learning, for many polytechnics and universities see the emphasis of our work purely on the recreational side and consequently make provision for the subject outside committed lecture time. It could be argued that our organised games are purely recreational and should not be included within school time. Professor Harold Vander Zwaag of the University of Massachusetts takes this stand and states, 'We think that during the school-day students should be involved only with those pursuits which are of an academic nature.'[1] From this statement he accepts sports skill classes but is against sports participation as such.

We would not wish our position in the school timetable to be maintained just by tradition, and in our best interests, we cannot argue that 'The inclusion of physical education as part of the school curriculum needs no justification.' Neither should we automatically consider that physical education is a subject of educational value. This point is well made by Jelfs who says, 'to assume that physical education is an area of educational activity is an assumption of immense proportions. . . .'[2] A confused position has been created and to an extent we are adding to the confusion by merely doing a good hard-working job with only vague aims and objectives in mind. Felshin expresses some disquiet about the whole position in the opening sentence of one of her books:

A characterisation of physical education and human movement

> Physical education is threatened from a number of sides. Its purpose is challenged, its cost questioned and its value doubted, but greater than any of these threats is the inability of its defenders to give effective expression to the essential vitality of its role in everyday life.[3]

In the school setting, the subject is almost entirely practically based. We are 'doers' and performers, producing skill and the application of the skill to the conditions of the activity. The usual styles of teaching are the command style, problem solving and individual programming. In the command style, the demonstration is all-important and the subsequent teaching attempts to mould each individual to the understood pattern. This approach looks orderly and organised, it tends to produce skill especially in the 11–13 age range but the method may be questioned educationally, and also because it is essentially teacher-dominated, it may be responsible for many of the problems that occur later on. The command style is authoritarian even though the commands may be presented in a pleasant enough fashion. The youngsters are strait-laced into doing things in a particular way which allows nothing for their real understanding of the activity, and their subsequent varied application of this knowledge. Those youngsters who find success in the system usually retain a full interest in physical education and acquire status as representative members of competitive teams. This is about 10 per cent. The rest often work half-heartedly through a series of what are termed recreation subjects, organised on short-term course bases and productive of uncertain results.

Women teachers have tended to be somewhat more experimental in teaching and have made much use of the problem solving style which lends itself well to educational gymnastics. In addition, individual programming has appeared in connection with modern educational dance and this style also has contributed to good understanding and good performance. In girls' schools, however, the casual organisation of recreative subjects has also crept in, with often the same ineffective results as has happened with the boys. Generally, we seem to be mixing up an educational approach with a recreational approach without being certain of the difference. The educational approach demands at least a reasonable understanding by the youngster of the total movement, an ability to apply certain mechanical principles, a practical knowledge of the development of the associated skills, particular ways of practice, ideas about motivation, social etiquettes and the spectator side. In contrast, a recreational emphasis may merely offer an easy way of 'how to' and some transitory enjoyment.

The physically educated youngster

In secondary school physical education, a youngster has courses lasting for five years, and it is doubtful if very much thought is given by the staff regarding the qualities and abilities of the final product. Five years of teaching should lead to a physically educated youngster who bears many hallmarks of his education. He should be able to stand alongside his peers taking 'O' level examinations with a relative ability and knowledge. Mosston would see the physically educated youngster as the 'free, independent person' who has been encouraged to understand and apply knowledge about physical education so that he can stand on his own two feet regarding decisions and actions, and is knowledgeable and practical in the subject.[4]

Whatever our approach, we must teach with quite definite aims and objectives in mind. These must not be vague or woolly but quite definitely stated and planned with care. Objectives must be associated with each separate course or with each term's work and they must refer to the starting point of the youngsters and the considered goal. This implies that we must regularly undertake evaluation although there may be objections to this because of its apparent time-consuming nature. However, unless we know existing standards and the outcome of our work we cannot be sure either of the efficiency of our teaching method or the adequacy of the curriculum content. Whether we like it or not, a continuous, purposeful process of evaluation must be established. Bookwalter says 'A field or profession is in part judged by its evaluative devices and their uses. Evaluation is an integral part of the educational process.'[5]

Evaluation in individual activities like athletics, swimming and gymnastics should not present great problems, and should be something where the youngster can co-operate by keeping a record on a prepared form. The form will contain information about his present standing, his aspired objectives, his programme of work and his practical evaluation at the end of the course.

Physical education in colleges

A reappraisal of our work in schools is not the only problem that has faced us recently for there have been enough changes going on since the early 1960s to merit calling the period a time of quiet revolution. Up to that time, physical education in colleges had been a straightforward professional subject concentrating on developing performers and providing information and practice on teaching method and curriculum content. With the prospect of BEd degrees, and a year to be spent for the most part in academic study, major plans were made for the new courses and these have tended to have repercussions throughout the whole field.

The BEd course allowed for a good hard look to be taken at the general understanding of theoretical aspects of physical education, concerning which there was unorganised and scant information rather than well-understood knowledge. There obviously was much discussion on all contributory subjects ranging from underlying problems that were philosophical, to general arguments about content and order of importance. Since the degree was in education, educational aspects of physical education was a compulsory section; three other sections had to be undertaken, chosen from kinesiology, evaluation, psychological aspects, social aspects, history and comparative, adapted and aesthetics. The various courses allowed for the development of some specialisation and gave opportunity for much deeper study in the subject, especially on the part of the staff. Physical education had taken a big step forward regarding general understanding and interpretation.

Movement studies

The momentum that had developed retained its impetus but at the same time serious criticisms were levelled at many parts of the subject. These criticisms became formulated into such questions as: Is the title of physical education meaningful? Have we a standing as an academic subject? Have we developed a proper body of knowledge? Have we definite aims as an educational subject? How do these new ideas affect the professional situation? The majority of these questions and criticisms are interlinked and are reflections on different emphases to the subject as a whole. The questions provide evidence of an attempt to plan a properly structured, educationally based, academically accepted, correctly titled subject. It clearly became obvious that from the breadth of options included in the BEd courses that progress had been made beyond the practical field of physical education, although this was not a denial of the place and importance of the practical. The subject had become the study of the phenomenon of human movement, of man in movement, in fact human movement studies or movement studies. A study of the subject would be wide ranging but would allow nevertheless for particular specialisms. The wide range or, as Curl states, 'the wide spectrum could include locomotive movements, gross operational movements, expression movements, athletic movements, balletic movements, dramatic movements and ritualistic movement'.[6] Each of these is a separate and distinct study of man in movement and each study must be considered and appraised in its own particular way. In this context Renshaw states,

> In each case the form of movement experience would contain its own unique features, its own mode of operation, its own standards of appraisal and its own criteria of appropriateness. Thus, different kinds of propositional knowledge (knowing that), practical knowledge (knowing how) and acquaintance knowledge would support each distinct action.[7]

It is essential that we are aware of the proper approach to each particular movement and that we can differentiate movements, allocate them into their correct form and then describe and interpret them accurately within that form. If the proper explanation is not given, this is what Ryle calls a 'myth' or 'the presentation of facts belonging to one category in the idiom of another'.[8]

There also must be a 'structure' or group of subjects which serve as explanatory to movement studies. Regarding such an explanation, Renshaw considers that

> the many different facets of human movement can be described, analysed and explained adequately only through the medium of three fundamental modes of thought—that is through philosophy (e.g. aesthetics and philosophical psychology), the physical sciences (e.g. kinesiology and biomechanics) and the human sciences (e.g. psychology, social psychology, sociology, cultural anthropology and history).[9]

Because several modes of thought are necessary the subject is termed a 'field of knowledge'; the field possesses its own internal coherence since the focal point is the explanation of human movement.

The structured approach to movement studies now presented allows for a real enrichment of the subject academically, professionally and in the school situation. Perhaps a bone of contention in the past had been the apparent lack of academic status, but with this new approach this problem may have been overcome.

Movement studies could be a university subject studied from a normal academic point of view. The course of study would be for intrinsic reasons aiming, amongst other things, for 'the development of certain qualities of mind, powers of reasoning and the capacity for general ideas'. . . .[10] The theoretical aspects, however, would have to be enriched by a certain amount of chosen practical work; this also would be for intrinsic development. Obviously, theoretical knowledge is not sufficient for the full appreciation of an academic course in a practically based subject.

The general approach suggested for academic study can to a large extent be transferred to teacher education. For some years now an important part of the work in colleges of education has been purely for personal or intrinsic development. In physical education this has hitherto applied to the practical aspect rather than to the theoretical side, but with greater emphasis on academic work a deeper study and a broad understanding of the subject as a whole could develop. Such a study would cover the structure of knowledge previously outlined and would make a student keenly aware of the basic philosophy and value of the subject.

The professional work associated with teaching would be developed to include new approaches that movement studies could make in the school situation. The subject has to take its place in the educational setting of the school, and consequently its value and its contribution to the educational development of the youngster must be understood in theory and application. This approach will considerably affect objectives, curriculum content and method of teaching, and should help to regularise work so that there is not a fall-away of interest in the upper age ranges of the school. Teaching methods which are educational, as distinct from coaching and training, must be understood, and ways developed of making the youngster a more important partner in the teacher-learner combination.

The wider aspects of college work could have repercussions in the school from a theoretical point of view, and the subject could be developed to include classroom lessons in addition to the present practical work. Projects on fitness, applied physiology, mechanics and skill development have already been carried out to a high level and with success in many schools and it is not difficult to extend these studies. New topics could include social aspects, aesthetics, expression and communication, adapted work, etc. It would appear that with a new approach to the understanding of movement studies, a different emphasis in the school setting and the enrichment of facilities that has taken place in the last few years, our place in education may be considerably enhanced.

Notes

1 H. J. Vander Zwaag, *Towards a Philosophy of Sport*, Addison-Wesley, 1972.
2 B. W. Jelfs, 'Thinking about the Meaning of Physical Education', *Brit. Journn. Phys. Ed.*, vol. 1, no. 6, November 1970.
3 J. Felshin, *Perspectives and Principles for Physical Education*, Wiley, 1967.
4 M. Mosston, *Teaching Physical Education*, Merrill, 1966.
5 K. Bookwalter and H. Vander Zwaag, *Foundations and Principles of Physical Education*, W. B. Saunders, 1969.
6 G. F. Curl, 'An Attempt to Justify Human Movement as a Field of Study' in J. D. Brooke and H. T. A. Whiting (eds), *Human Movement: A Field of Study*, Henry Kimpton, 1973.
7 P. Renshaw, 'An Analytical Approach to Education and Physical Education' in *Education and Physical Education—Conference Report, 1972*, pub. Nonington College.
8 G. Ryle, *The Concept of Mind*, Peregrine, 1949.
9 P. Renshaw, 'Human Movement Studies and the Curriculum'—unpublished paper, University of Leeds.
10 *Ibid.*

2

Towards a dynamic and objective theory of movement studies

R. L. Groves

When the McNair report on teacher training was published in 1944 it recommended that the study of a main field course should be pursued for personal development rather than professional competence. This meant that physical education had to face up to the challenge of preparing syllabuses suitable for intellectual appraisal, for in those early days these courses did not rise far beyond the technology of teaching, while matters relating to a wider perspective of sport and movement received very little attention. Since that time, the subject has made considerable progress in assembling a body of knowledge from several sources to illuminate our understanding of physical activity in our culture. Two significant milestones in this development have been the acceptance of physical education as part of the BEd degree structure and, at least in London, a change of name to movement studies (Hinks *et al.*, 1971). Both these moves, at the level of higher education, are an indication of an ambition to inculcate in students a good instrumental preparation supported by a background of theory which 'fosters their imagination, sensitivities, critical powers and social consciences, so that they begin to come to terms with the situation in which they are placed as human beings' (Peters, 1973).

My intention is to reconsider the standards and criteria which structure the various levels of our work and the consequences of their influence, for I believe we have reached a time when it is necessary to emphasise the independent aspects of the subject and to clarify the relationship of movement to movement studies. The thought which prompts this inquiry is that, partly because of our essential pursuit for parity in higher education, we have so far followed a course which is separating the theory from the practical to such an extent that one is failing to influence the other. This division is doubly unfortunate because it occurs at a time when the 'accelerative thrust' of progress is breaking down the boundaries within and between communities, and new ideas are needed to facilitate adaptions to changing circumstances (Schon, 1971; Toffler, 1970).

It is precisely this predicament of understanding the possible and various contributions of physical achievement, physical recreation and physical education that makes it desirable to monitor continually the trends in these areas. Initially, games, as formalised in the public schools, satisfied all the conditions in these areas simultaneously. The dominant interest of the masters, however, was the use of sport as a substantial part of a strong appeal to conform to a particular set of rules (Howarth, 1973). From this beginning modern sport has grown tremendously in popularity and, as I have noted elsewhere, established many different standards (Groves, 1972). Nowadays, approximately one hundred years after the creation of the official Sports Associations, physical activity is shaped by complex and sometimes conflicting hierarchies of values, with the priority given to winning, sportsmanship, exercise or excellence, producing qualitative changes in the play.

J. White (1973) is well wide of the mark when he states, in his attempts to classify the essential and non-essential parts of the curriculum, that the concepts appropriate to games can be learned without actually taking part in the game. An observer would soon understand how the game is organised, but the real meaning of the play, as determined by the players' judgments and perceptions, would escape notice and he would never understand the players on their terms. Learning how to play games involves more than action; inevitably it also involves experiencing and respecting how it is valued by others. Furthermore, as far as education is concerned, it requires some understanding of the rules which have been accepted as the basis for interpersonal relationships on the field of play.

What J. White superciliously calls 'the contemporary malaise in the physical education profession' (p. 42) is not simply the result of an attempt to show that 'movement studies' is academically respectable, although this objective has to be considered. The subject is young, and where it has been troubled by acne the blemishes are not always due to internal disorders. Very often they are caused by demands insisting that its sub-domains become 'scientific' or 'academic' before they relate to the problems in sport and recreation. In this respect those disciplines associated with social studies (and possibly J. White) should sympathise with our problems. But more often than not they repeat the criticisms they had to endure in their early days, and these tender memories make them tyrannical parents—at least that is how it often appears.

My contention is that the main substance of the work in movement studies should be orientated towards searching for the essential features of the several rapidly changing value systems that interact with various levels of participation in sport, creative movement and other forms of active leisure. These aspects should be investigated because, like Everest, they are there, but more importantly, because they determine life styles, and how they evolve will influence the climate of a dominant area of everyday society. Movement studies does not possess an exclusive right to this interest. In an age, however, when nations, sports associations, councils, businesses and the mass-media control most of the outward appearances of play, the case for a relatively disinterested and intense examination of the place of physical activity in the community is not without some support. The main function of the subject should, therefore, be a critical one, pointing out contradictions that exist and adjudicating between the theories which seek to determine the future of sport and recreation.

With regard to physical education, out of which movement studies is growing, this critical faculty has been muffled by an exaggerated and apologetic concern for objectives which place the subject within an acceptable framework of education. What has emerged is a consensus of ideas that discourages an argumentative stance towards accepted practices. For example, the last really significant reconstruction of what is actually taught took place near the end of the Second World War. In the primary school the child-centred philosophy proved to be an ideal setting for the ideas expressed in *Moving and Growing* (Ministry of Education, 1952). Children were, therefore, exhorted to explore, experiment and invent movements; several links with other subjects were established also, so that many worthwhile and interesting projects could be planned. An equally large reconstruction at secondary level was made possible by the rejection of first, formal, unimaginative gymnastic exercises and, second, the belief that qualities experienced on the sports field transferred to everyday life. From this moment men's and women's work diverged, with the former electing to concentrate on the teaching of a wide range of skills as a preparation for post-school recreation, and the latter accepting the idea of Laban's Motion factors as being the foundation to all movement training. This divergence precipitated a lively dialogue about the need for 'skill' or 'skills'. However, over the past thirty years the more excessive claims on both sides have been either modulated or modified and the differences between them are now fairly small.

The crucial point is that the full benefit of the work in the primary school has not been felt, largely because there is a lack of teachers who can teach the subject. Apart from a few outstanding examples, the lessons I see resemble a bedlam of uninspired activity which satisfy neither the teacher nor the child. The theory appears to be good, but the application needs more attention. In the secondary schools the position is reversed in that what good work there is goes on in spite of an adequate frame of reference. The recreative approach imposes few limits on what is taught and the movement approach, based on a dogmatic unfalsifiable theory, is equally resistant to criticism.

The depressingly poor standards in too many of our schools are not peculiar to physical education, and there is a fairly general demand for a radical reformation of the curriculum. But, if physical education continues to stand apart from the critical debates that seek to disentangle the impending changes imposed by circumstances on the whole educational system, it will be overwhelmed by these events and suffer the incomprehensible stresses that accompany a failure to respond to change. The subject ought to be involved, for example, in the debate about an alternative to the 'watered-down' academic timetable that is impairing the personalities of the majority of adolescent children. One suggestion by Bantock (1971) awards a high priority to movement in an education through the emotions. Although, personally, I find it difficult to accept his retention of the broad but inflexible bands which offer to one group a 'cognitive-intellectual' education, and to the other an 'affective-artistic' education. Surely, this is no more than a reproduction of something that has been tried before and found inadequate!

What education and physical education require, if they are to satisfy various ages and abilities, is a flexible organisation which makes external standards subservient to the particular needs of a person.

There are, I believe some cogent arguments for replacing the traditional monolithic timetable with a series of networks which ensure that the person is at the centre of a process allowing him to work outwards towards standards which contribute to self-esteem and to his understanding of the world. One such largely non-prescriptive approach to the curriculum has been proposed by James (1969) and Mason (1970). They appeal for a fourfold curriculum which allows a child to plan, in consultation with a member of staff, a programme of learning which includes personal interests, class involvement and work not normally included in schools. A more extreme model, incorporating the same ideas, has been outlined by Illich (1971). He suggests schools are a dangerous substitute for education. All that a pupil needs are four resources to help him define and achieve his own goals: they are, first, a reference service to laboratories, libraries, museums, rental agencies, etc.; second, access to people willing to serve as models for others who wish to learn the skills they possess; third, a matching service which enables people with similar interests to meet; and fourth, professional tutors, to assist learners and to administer the other three resources. The new community schools projects (ILEA, 1973), incidentally, with their desire to involve parents and local centres in the life and work of the children, may strike a reasonable balance between these two ideas. Inevitably they will initiate new methods and thereby add a new dimension to schooling by creating a new set of problems to solve.

How is physical education to adjust to similar situations? As a matter of fact some of the new problems are already nibbling away at the traditional presentation of the subject in the form of 'dual use' of facilities and the employment of non-qualified teachers. For my part, I am in favour of these developments, but I also think that the lack of clear educational guidelines makes it even more likely that children will be used as the toys or tools of a teacher/instructor. Moreover, the little attention given to these changes will, if the profession is not alert, ensure that the important decisions will be taken by others and the educational significance of the changes will be buried beneath more pragmatic assumptions.

In an attempt to distinguish what is an appropriate structure for personal growth, Groves and Hancock (1974) have outlined a psychological model for individual behaviour. They review the literature which suggests that perceptions are shaped and selected by previous experiences and conclude that a truly objective appraisal of the environment is a rare event. These writers trace how this notion of personal responsibility for interpreting the world has received spasmodic attention throughout the history of psychology, and comment upon the assumptions which place this idea within a viable form of education. The idea is that people categorise events in order to make sense of what they perceive and they plan their future according to mental schemes (Bartlett, 1932), frames of mind (Hudson, 1968), or personal constructs (Kelly, 1963). All these descriptions refer to the mental strategies people use to create their personal reality, which embraces their total self and their relationship with other people. These strategies do not depend on the ability to verbalise, nor are they necessarily simple structures; they are, however, given non-threatening conditions, the means by which a person experiments with life and moves towards becoming a fully functioning member of society. In their synthesis of this essentially Humanistic concept of a person they suggest that G. A. Kelly's personal construct theory is the most important because 'it embraces the spirit of the previous work in this area and provides the crucial balance between crediting a person with control over his future, and a means of appraising the dimensions that shape his temporary reality' (Groves and Hancock, 1974).

The importance of this approach to physical education is that external standards for movement, although important, are merely the means of helping a person explore the relevance of his environment and to make value judgments. The real emphasis should be upon the personal qualities that arise out of participation. It is, if I dare mention it, a more discriminating perspective on the character-forming objective of the pre-war era, in the sense that it seeks to promote an orderly, imaginative and structurally conceived quality of mind. At a minimal level of acceptance it does, at least, offer an antidote to the contemporary 'individualistic programmes' emanating from America, heavy with such words as response, reinforcement, rewards, schedules and behaviour modification (Rushall and Siendeltop, 1972).

In what ways does physical education create pathways which could facilitate the development of an integrated, fully functioning person? Well, as an interim, purely speculative suggestion, an arrangement of our objectives could be made to fit a series of developmental levels through which a person might progress on his way to maturity. The route will not appeal to everyone, but for those who start by taking physical activity as a dominant value and want to change their standpoint later, there are multiple points of departure leading to new interests. Each level would serve as a foundation for new perceptions, new evolvements and new anticipations which highlight the characteristics of the next. Briefly the increases in self-development associated with standards in movement to structure one's pursuits would divide, I believe, into four distinct phases. The first would be the *play phase* with the accent on the experience of movement for its own sake. The justification for this phase would be quite simply the muscular sensuousness that results from exercise. The pleasure gained would ensure repetition and, in a stimulating environment, further exploration of the essential components of intelligence, self-assertion and skill. Second would be the *educational phase* in which a person learns the rules of the game and the codes of behaviour which are acceptable in his Societies. Learning is mainly by example and imitation in structured situations which are intrinsically satisfying. In this phase physical activities should be adapted, as in the case of educational gymnastics for example, to assist in the construction of a self-image (Mead, 1934) and, for example, in the case of educational games, to assist in the learning of how to make moral judgments (Piaget, 1960). In a Utopian state (as perhaps some people regarded the Victorian Public Schools) there would be few conflicting values and people would not be encouraged to review their conception of the world. Indeed, Skinner (1972) seems to suggest that most people still should not rise beyond such a given state if we wish to ensure their happiness and the survival of a culture which he has defined. His proposal for a scientific analysis of behaviour in order to elucidate laws which would create this uncritical state of affairs appears, however, to depreciate people, and therefore, as a final objective, to be the opposite of a good education. None the less, it is almost inevitable that the basic ethical and social principles of groups are experienced and used before they are questioned. There is, of course, no guarantee that the values which underpin one area of life will serve as a guideline for another—but some values will be absorbed into the very 'core' of a personality to form fairly stable parts of a philosophy of life; the importance of sport as a cultural force merely stresses that conduct should be judged by reference to a sportsman's code of ethics.

The third phase relates to an *aesthetic* approach to aspects of games or movement. This could range in quality from a fairly indiscriminating, and perhaps vicarious, pleasure to a peak experience originating from either the performance of a skilled activity, or a critical appreciation that transcends the functional effectiveness of the movement. In other words, this emotion could express itself in cognitive, conative or affective terms (Maslow, 1970). Maheu (1963) is despondent that sport has not inspired other art forms to capture its spirit, but most sportsmen are content to regard sport as an independent vehicle for the display of artistic ability. Without any doubt, when movement lacks this quality its appeal is reduced to a laborious, mechanical routine.

In a previous attempt to discover the most likely explanation for both the theory and practice of movement, this phase was considered to be the most relevant (Carlisle, 1969). My thought is that while this phase appropriately describes and appreciates skilled acts, a further dimension is necessary if progress is not to be arrested by an ardent admiration of the existing expressions of skill. Moreover, if movement is exclusively categorised in this area, it too quickly becomes abstracted from the private fund of personal and implicit experience (Polanyi, 1958 and 1967), and is transformed by study into something very different.

So far, I have tried to describe how movement experience can be adapted to particular phases of growth in order to assist in the process of developing an expanding and transforming sense of self. The training in skill, therefore, is always conducted against a background which defines the value systems of all the participants. If the aim is to assist in the formation of independent and mature minds, subjective beliefs have to be raised to a level where they can probe and explore the habitual characteristics of sport and sportsmen. Movement studies has made some considerable progress towards categorising the appropriate research and literature, but it has not always been able to justify adequately what should be its distinguishing characteristic, that is, a link that directly connects practical sporting activity with the various disciplines that influence our understanding. Thus, F. Henry's (1964) affirmation that physical educationists are like the biochemists who are neither biologists nor chemists has been a vision not fully realised. The lack of this link means that the shift from practice to theory, from private to shared knowledge, is unco-ordinated. As a consequence the forms of knowledge within our field tend to be developed autonomously, growing outwards like spokes on a rimless wheel. A further weakness with this type of structure is created by the tendency to use the questions, as well as the techniques, from other study areas, perhaps long after they have ceased to be the main topics of discussion in the appropriate disciplines. Students of movement are thereby committed to intellectualising without a serious problem.

Without a rational synthesising unit to identify and investigate some of the concrete problems arising out of sport, creative movement and recreative pursuits, the subject is unable to establish a truly reciprocating relationship with either physical activity or other subjects. In this respect our attempts to fit into Hirst's (1965) classifications of knowledge may have overrun their full course. Further adaptations might well be counter-productive in that the outcome will be a conforming, fragmented field of study in the no-man's-land between scholarship and sporting performance.

There is no doubt that the concept of 'forms' and 'fields' of study has influenced the subject's growth. In the final analysis, however, the study of movement is an applied subject and an intelligent appraisal of practical issues is not an optional extra. Hirst actually makes this point in an article about the professional preparation of graduates for teaching, when he writes: 'Practical grasp must go hand in hand with theoretical understanding. Theory divorced from practice in the exercise of skills, will remain inapplicable theory, for applying theory is itself an art' (Hirst, 1974).

The question of constructing an over-arching structure concerned with a rational investigation of specific problems is, I submit, most essential. Without this element the subject has no cutting edge, and sport, especially championship sport, may find that it is difficult to explain the relevance of its procedures in a rapidly changing society. But if we add such a structure to the present design of courses the ritual, pre-theoretical and subconscious practices deeply embedded in the character of institutions and sportsmen can be laid bare and subjected to analysis. In so doing it will add to sport a liberalising spirit by providing a stable foundation for 'socratic' dialogues between Associations and Athletes, Society and Sportsmen and, not least, sporting self and other aspects of self. Moreover, students of this new element, which for the time being I shall call 'political studies in sport and recreation' (to signify that it is broader than education studies and more firmly based) will, it is hoped, influence the growth of active leisure by adopting an informed, questioning openmindedness to their involvement in these affairs. They, more than any other group, should become the emancipated inheritors of the qualities that were once the exclusive prerogative of the 'gentleman-amateur'.

The scientific method proposed by Popper is most appropriate to this discussion. His fundamental thesis is as follows:

> The way in which knowledge progresses, and especially our scientific knowledge, is by unjustified (and unjustifiable) anticipations, by guesses, by tentative solutions to our problems, by conjectures. These conjectures are controlled by criticism; that is, by attempted refutations, which include severely critical tests. They may survive these tests; but they can never be positively justified; they can neither be established as certain nor even as probable (in the sense of probability calculus). Criticism of our conjectures is of decisive importance; by bringing out our mistakes it makes us understand the difficulties of the problem which we are trying to solve. This is how we become better acquainted with our problem, and able to propose more mature solutions; the very refutation of a theory—that is, of any serious tentative solution to our problem—is always a step forward that takes us nearer the truth. This is how we learn from our mistakes (Popper, 1963).

This idea is advanced one step further in a later book which demonstrates how subjective beliefs can be translated into objective knowledge by expressing them in the form of statements which are susceptible to criticism (Popper, 1972). In this way man can scientifically examine the rules and practices which direct the planned and unplanned consequences of play. Science, in this context, is essentially a discipline invented by men to help them formulate more helpful understanding of the forces which constrain human and social action. The thought that suggests that the dominant features in man and society are universal laws which can be predicted and controlled is replaced by the thought that man, by his own efforts, constructs the rules of work and play.

When this view of objective knowledge is associated with personal knowledge as exemplified by, for example, George Kelly, it is possible to forge the cutting edge that movement studies needs. It can then pare away the general assumptions that often excuse men from accepting responsibility for the beliefs which determine a given culture. Within the broad framework that movement studies has developed an approach of this kind should spin the thread to hold the subject together. Where this thread is missing there is always the danger that the really important problems will exist outside the range of the study areas and that the scientific aspects, in particular, will produce a mechanistic account of human performance.

As it now stands a student of movement studies lacks the means of bridging the gap between theory and practice. He is often left with the impression that what he studies is knowledge for its own sake. Furthermore it is frequently difficult for him to integrate the learning that goes on in different study areas. Indeed, a good case can be argued for progress along these lines up to the present time (i.e. 1974). But further growth requires more than an appreciation of theory and practice. Both sides must interact continuously if they are to remain sensitive to the needs of people and society.

The creation of a link study building on the unstable system of attitudes, values and ambitions which determine the quality of play could add this new dimension by constructively criticising movement, by proposing solutions to problems, by defining new questions for the disciplines to answer and by making people aware of the possibilities they can activate. More importantly it would teach students/players how to monitor their own actions and help them avoid being the victims of inheritance and circumstances. Such a creation would not only strike up a reciprocating relationship between knowledge and experience, but would also start a new phase in the evolution of the subject and thereby assist in the development of an objective, dynamic and relevant area of study.

References

Bantock, G. W. (1971), 'Towards a Theory of Popular Education', in R. Hooper, ed. *The Curriculum Context, Design and Development*, Open University, Oliver & Boyd, Edinburgh.

Bartlett, F. X. (1932), *Remembering*, Cambridge University Press.

Carlisle, R. (1969), 'The Concept of Physical Education', in *Proceedings of Annual Conference, Philosophy of Education Society of Great Britain.*

Groves, R. (1972), 'Physical Education, Recreation and Competitive Sport', in *Bulletin of Physical Education*, July, vol. IX, no. 3, pp. 33–8.

Groves, R. and Hancock, J. (1974), 'A Search for the Person in Educational Practice; a Psychological Viewpoint, in *Transcript*, no. 6 (1975), Garnett College, London.

Henry, F. (1964), 'Physical Education—An Academic Discipline', in the leaflet (PEA) January–February 1965.
Hinks, E. M., Archbutt, S. E. and Curl, G. F. (1971), 'Movement Studies; a new Standing Committee', in *Bulletin, University of London Institute of Education*, no. 23, spring term.
Hirst, P. (1965), 'Liberal Education and the Nature of Knowledge', in R. D. Archambault (ed.), *Philosophical Analysis and Education*, Routledge & Kegan Paul.
Hirst, P. (1974), 'Professional preparation', in *TES*, March, no. 3,069, p. 21.
Howarth, P. (1973), *Play up and Play the Game*, Eyre Methuen.
Hudson, L. (1968), *Frames of Mind*, Methuen.
ILEA (1973), *An Education Service for the whole Community; a Joint Report of the Further and Higher Education Sub-Committee and the Schools Sub-Committee*, ILEA.
Illich, I. D. (1971), *Deschooling Society*, Calder & Boyars Ltd.
James, C. (1969), *Young Lives at Stake; a Reappraisal of Secondary Schools*, Collins.
Kelly, G. A. (1963), *A Theory of Personality; The Psychology of Personal Constructs*, Norton.
Maheu, R. (1963), 'Sport and Culture', in *Revue Analytique d'Education Physique et Sportive*, vol. 5, no. 2, pp. 156–66, ICSPE.
Maslow, A. H. (1970, rev. ed.), *Motivation and Personality*, Harper & Row.
Mason, E. A. (1970), *Collaborative Learning*, Ward Lock Educational.
McNair, A. (1944), *Teachers and Youth Leaders, Report to Board of Education*, HMSO.
Mead, C. H. (1934), *Mind, Self and Society*, University of Chicago Press.
Ministry of Education (1952), *Physical Education in the Primary School, Part I, Moving and Growing*, HMSO.
Peters, R. (1973), 'Farewell to Aims', in 'Aims of Education; an Interdisciplinary Inquiry', *London Educational Review*, Autumn, vol. 2, no. 3.
Piaget, J. (1960), *The Moral Judgment of the Child*, Routledge & Kegan Paul.
Polanyi, M. (1958), *Personal Knowledge*, Routledge & Kegan Paul.
Polanyi, M. (1967), *The Tacit Dimension*, Routledge & Kegan Paul.
Popper, K. R. (1963), *Conjectures and Refutations,* Routledge & Kegan Paul.
Popper, K. R. (1972), *Objective Knowledge; An Evolutionary Approach*, Oxford University Press.
Rushall, B. S. and Siendeltop, D. (1972), *Development and Control of Behaviour in Sport and Physical Education*, Lea & Febiger.
Russell, B. (1946), *A History of Western Philosophy*, Allen & Unwin.
Schon, D. A. (1971), *Beyond the Stable State*, Temple Smith.
Skinner, B. F. (1972), *Beyond Freedom and Dignity*, Jonathan Cape.
Toffler, A. (1970), *Future Shock*, Bodley Head.
White, J. (1973), *Towards a Compulsory Curriculum*, Routledge & Kegan Paul.

3

Movement as an art form

S. E. Archbutt

Man, existing within a complex physical framework, has many needs and desires. In order to survive he must identify these, think how to satisfy them and then act. Action means movement, and how he uses movement must vary according to its purpose and the situation.

Movement is used in practical working actions to contribute to the routine of sustaining life and providing the physical necessities of food, water, warmth, cleanliness and protection. From birth man also uses movement as a gesture language to help to communicate his needs to others, for he is unable to survive alone. Man reacts emotionally to everything in his environment, especially in relation to whether his needs and desires are satisfied. Tensions built up through negation, repression and conflict, whether of physical or mental origin, must be released if he is to function harmoniously. Movement is used for the expression of such passions and emotions. Man also has the gift of play. This enables him to set up synthetic situations which he uses to sublimate and temper his emotional reactions, extend himself beyond the actual life situation in which he finds himself and develop his practical imagination and thought. In play movement is again used, for a variety of purposes. Man uses it in this context to assist growth and maintain his capacity to function as fully as possible, to examine and gain understanding of his environment, to make contact with and relate to other people, to restore his physical and mental balance, to heighten his personal awareness and prowess, and to continually re-assess his own powers of survival and status.

Most human beings also have the urge to do more than exist,

grow, communicate their needs, vent their emotions and play. They are curious and continually seek new experiences, to provide new challenges and delight the senses. More than this, they have the capacity to marvel and wonder at things they find of beauty and interest, the urge to extend and give pleasurable sensations as well as receive them, and the urge to create for themselves an ideal environment. Man thinks about his experiences and feelings and has the strong desire to record and symbolise his emotions and the powers he feels to be at work in the universe, to communicate these feelings and share them with others. Here again he uses movement to fulfil a purpose. He uses it to create, not for the mere pleasure of the process, but because he desires to share a vision, a thought, an aesthetic sensation, to beautify his world, to lead a richer and fuller life. He finds everyday language insufficient to communicate these kinds of thoughts and feelings, so he takes all kinds of materials and builds, moulds and transforms them, creating shapes, colours, textures, sounds and movements, which become symbols of his joy, amusement, sorrow, awe and reverence. The works which result express his urge for harmonious organisation, for form, design, unity, co-operation. They express his appetite for fantasy, his vision of beauty, his wonder at the strange and unfamiliar, his search for profundity and the truths of his universe, his sense of humour, his delight in skill, his desire to share and give pleasure and thanks for what his spirit has gained. Movement as an art form is used to this end.

Movement as an art form is often regarded as synonymous with dancing, and it is certainly in forms of poetic and dramatic dance expression that it can achieve its fullest potential of communication. Here it can stand comparison with the other arts in depth, range, complexity and skill, and in its capacity to provoke thought, provide insight, move one emotionally, stir the imagination and produce aesthetic satisfaction. Dancing, however, can take many forms and be used for other purposes: for erotic play, personal display, physical exercise, social accomplishment; to achieve ecstasy and trance or acrobatic skill; as part of religious ritual; or to serve educational ends.

Other activities, such as gymnastics, ice-skating and swimming may reveal a certain degree of artistic intent and cause one to marvel at the skill of the performers. They are certainly carried beyond the bounds of necessity or play. To be used fully as art forms, however, these activities are often limited by being used as competitive sports, or by an over-emphasis on skill for its own sake, or by lack of use to convey thought, or touch the spectator emotionally. This is not to say that they cannot give aesthetic pleasure. Aesthetic reaction can be the result of anything in nature, work, play or art which causes an onlooker to appreciate materials, living things, sounds, movements, for their forms, colours, shapes, textures, rhythms alone. But art forms are intended by man to evoke and express more than purely aesthetic reaction. He strives to communicate his deeper feelings, ideas and thoughts about the world, in a way relative to their importance to him and to his respect for and desire to be respected by other men.

Artistic intent may be evidenced at different levels, from that of the child to that of the mature, professional artist. It is not solely the province of those who have already achieved a high degree of technical skill. Art is a process of increasing discovery and achievement in the service of a spiritual aim. Dreams, emotion and willpower alone, however, will not further this aim. To work in any artistic medium can be exciting and produce moments of joy and satisfaction, but the artist must undergo discipline, struggle, criticism and moments of despair. The movement artist uses special bodily tensions, attitudes, movement shapes and rhythms and links them in a distinctive, unbroken flow, which must hold the attention over a period of time until the full completion of the image he wishes to convey. He must train his body instrument so that it will be able to produce the effects he wishes, discover the possibilities and limitations of his medium, learn to work with a group, learn to grasp an idea and respond imaginatively and with practical sense, learn to understand the relationship between kinaesthetic experience and visual effect, and be prepared to learn from the ideas, methods and achievements of others. Movement artists may be performers, performer/composers or choreographers.

When looking at art, to complete the communicative process, attention and an effort of understanding is necessary on the part of the spectator, whether he be in a theatre audience, a teacher watching a student, or a child watching the work of another child. In this sense movement as an art form is a language, a symbolic language. It may be profound, playful, decorative, skilful, exciting, disturbing, ingenious, humorous, beautiful, in either simple or highly complex form. However, although art may entertain and delight, this is not its prime purpose. It is a sharing of thoughts and feelings, and the discovery that effort, skill and creation can uplift, harmonise and beautify. As such it is of utmost importance for the human soul, in a world of depressing news, discordant acts and ugly environments.

Participating in artistic activity can be educational in the fullest sense, provided that it is able to be carried through with integrity, and knowledgeable guidance is available. There is much ignorance of the value of education through art in our society, where material goals are so generally regarded as the means to a fuller life. This is reflected in the school curriculum and the time, facilities and status given to artistic activity. There is mild interest, but little deep belief in the value of the arts, or effort to understand the contribution they can make.

Movement used as a creative art experience can, perhaps, make a greater contribution than any other form of physical activity used in the educational context. The education of the body to move as a skilful instrument through gymnastics and dance assists harmonious growth and physical health and confidence. The awareness of movement in terms of shape, quality, relationship and meaning, gained through kinaesthetic feeling and observation of movement, carries through into an awareness, understanding, appraisal and appreciation of movement behaviour of all kinds in the total environment. The acts of co-operation, understanding, discipline, sharing, response, leadership, helping, necessary in group movement participation and creation, promote constructive social attitudes. The aim is not to beat or outwit, but to increase one's skill and the quality of one's personal contribution to the whole idea. There is a constant interplay of mind and body in qualitative movement charged with reflective emotional content, in an act of creation with a spiritual, communicative aim. This provides an outlet for emotional tension in a constructive, energetic form, enlivening as it releases, increasing the capacity to become fully absorbed and involved in whatever one does.

The concept and discussion of movement as an art form in the context of general education is a comparatively recent development in this country (post 1940). In practice it is revealed in the type of modern educational dance and modern educational gymnastics which have developed in our schools and colleges of education over the last thirty years. The ideas of Rudolf Laban (1879–1958) stand out as the major influence on a revolutionary shift of approach towards movement in education. Given initial impetus by the interest of a number of women physical educationists, grants awarded by the Ministry of Education from 1948 enabled deeper study at the Art of Movement Studio. Laban's work must be viewed in the context of that of other twentieth-century pioneers in the dance world in Europe and the USA, who reacted against existing forms, attempting to rediscover the essential movement substance of the dance, to revitalise and restore it to a position of respect and dignity as a major art and cultural influence. All their efforts reveal a search for deeper co-ordination of bodily action with movements of the intellectual, emotional and spiritual nature, to be manifested in a new approach to dance form, content and training. Laban's approach to the analysis of movement itself, the breadth of his interest in human effort and its movement manifestations in different spheres, the content and manner of his writings, and his invention of a more comprehensive movement notation system, opened doors to the possibility of a different type of approach to movement study, with both artistic and scientific significance.

The theoretical background to contemporary practice and understanding of movement as an art form is gradually being consolidated, as a result of academic questioning. There is investigation into how far inspirations and beliefs are supported by systematic evidence and logical argument. Notions and practices are now questioned from many viewpoints, scientific, aesthetic, psychological, social, historical, educational. The subject is vast, and the implications, ramifications and interconnections of the topics it impinges upon are only just beginning to be explored in depth and subjected to more general scrutiny in this country, as a result of the emergence of degree-level work in a subject gaining a new title, Movement Studies.

It must be remembered, however, that no amount of pure theorising will produce a work of art, or enable people to enter the world of creative art experience. The world of movement as an art form, at its highest and deepest, is ultimately the world of the professional artists and teachers who make its practice their life's work.

Bibliography

Cohen, S. J. (ed.) (1966), *The Modern Dance: Seven Statements of Belief*, Connecticut, Wesleyan University Press.

Coton, A. V. (1946), *The New Ballet*, London, Dobson.

Dewey, J. (1934), *Art as Experience*, New York, Capricorn.
Hawkins, A. M. (1964), *Creating Through Dance*, New Jersey, Prentice-Hall.
D'Houbler, M. (1962), *Dance, A Creative Art Experience*, Madison, University of Wisconsin Press.
Laban, R. (1948), *Modern Educational Dance*, London, Macdonald & Evans.
Laban, R. (1950), *The Mastery of Movement on the Stage*, London, Macdonald & Evans.
Langer, S. (1953), *Feeling and Form*, London, Routledge & Kegan Paul.
Langer, S. (1957), *Problems of Art*, New York, Scribners.
Lawson, J. (1964), *A History of Ballet and its Makers*, London, Pitman.
Leatherman, L. (1961), *Martha Graham*, London, Faber & Faber.
Martin, J. (1933), *The Modern Dance*, New York, A. & S. Barnes.
Metheny, E. (1968), *Movement and Meaning*, New York, McGraw-Hill.
Read, H. (1943), *Education Through Art*, London, Faber & Faber.
Redfern, H. B. (1973), *Concepts in Modern Educational Dance*, London, Henry Kimpton.
Reid, L. A. (1969), *Meaning in the Arts*, London, Allen & Unwin.
Sheets, M. (1966), *The Phenomenology of Dance*, Madison, University of Wisconsin Press.
Sorell, W. (1967), *The Dance Has Many Faces*, London, Thames & Hudson.
Van Praagh, P. and Brinson, P. (1963), *The Choreographic Art*, London, A. & C. Black.
Wigman, M. (1966), *The Language of Dance*, London, Macdonald & Evans.

Part 2

Movement, language and communication

4

Movement as a mode of communication and implications for teaching

M. J. Cooper

> Movement is one of man's languages and as such should be consciously mastered.
>
> (Laban, 1966)

One of the aims of this chapter is to show the significance of movement as one of man's languages and its integral relationship with his other modes of communication. Teacher of movement studies have unique opportunity for fostering in the children they teach one of the fundamental aspects of life—the ability to communicate. Communication is essential in the establishment of human relationships; it forms the structure of belonging to a community and the means to be understood and accepted by others. Children normally arrive at school with a repertoire of communication skills. A knowledgeable teacher will build on this basis, enhancing and developing more skilful, varied and adaptable approaches through situations requiring sensitive interactions both at a personal level and through the transmitting and receiving of information in all the aspects of movement. A teacher watching children communicate sees a continuous flow of behaviour. Speech may be involved—certainly movement will be evident, perhaps in the way the head tilts; the movement of hands and arms in gesture; the pattern of the bodily attitude balancing on one foot and then the other; perhaps a change in sitting position. There appear to be phases when movement only appears to be the communicating medium, from the very subtle changes in eye movement (Argyle, 1964) to the change of the whole bodily attitude (Lamb, 1965). Stance and posture reveal moods and emotions perhaps to an extent only realised by those who have studied the significance. Teachers of movement studies should have this knowledge. Professional actors, dancers and deaf people especially look for cues and signals not always noted by other people. Movement can be as effective as speech, and sometimes more so in communicating information influencing the perceptions of others. 'The whole body is an instrument for communication. The mode of expression is a visual act communicating the meaning by direct presentations' (Phenix, 1964).

There are times when the child interchanges the relationships of speech and movement as well as using them together, to communicate his thoughts in interaction with other people.

Argyle (1964) set out the following pattern of movement and language relationships:

1 Before speech is present movement and/or sounds communicate and there is action stress.
2 Words and movement are interchangeable languages with words colouring movements, or movement adding description to speech.
3 Speech finally becomes the primary means of communication and expression with movement taking a secondary part. In adults behaviour is variable at this stage, some show economy of gesture and imperceptible movements which shadow their main actions, others appear to gain verbal fluency through accompanying motion.

However speech, it is now known, even when it is apparently the only mode of communication, is accompanied by synchronised patterns of movement. It has been found that through a linguistic-kinesic analysis of behaviour even newborn infants show 'units of body motion which occur in ordered relationship to units of adult speech' (Condon, 1974). Indeed, Condon goes further and has observed that in any conversation the involved persons are establishing an intricate communicating dance interrelated in visual and auditory stimuli.

The further investigation of movement and its relationship with language will be discussed later when considering the implications for the learning/teaching situation but the need for further investigation by teachers of movement studies would add weight to the findings of researchers.

In the light of such a finding the teacher concerned with

movement studies, from the nursery school to the sec school, should be aware of the possibilities for the development movement as a means of communication and the enhancement of all the work through the knowledge of modes of transmitting and receiving information. The development of language has long been the concern of the teacher as the prime symbolism of thought. It is essential that teachers of movement studies see the need for the same logical planning and research into the significance of movement work with children, not as opposed to language but within its own right and as an integrated mode of communication with language. 'Practice in the varied and subtle arts of bodily expression is also needed if a person is to articulate non-discursive as well as discursive means' (Phenix, 1964). The interrelationships of language and movement experience, each adding to the understanding of the other, may be seen as a new approach to the young child's understanding of language, and/or, action based on words concepts, e.g. the words under and over, high and low, forwards and backwards, inside and outside have obvious leads for structured movement experience as well as for the acquiring of word concepts.

In school the teacher can provide throughout the day, as well as in specific movement sessions, the practice and consolidation of communication skills, as well as providing opportunities for further learning and development in the understanding of the subtleties of meaning through movement. The teacher needs to be alert during the day's programme for the moments of helping, guiding, questioning, coaching, and all the other aspects of teaching during the transmitting and receiving of information. The senses of touch, audition and vision should be focused on activities, and the communication of information through the sensory modes will be heightened if the teacher is aware of their boundless possibilities for learning. The sense of touch of blind children is usually far more sophisticated and sensitive as a means of receiving information than that of normal children. The teacher of movement studies should decide whether this level of sensitivity can be developed in all the senses for normal children.

Dr B. Tizzard in a lecture at the London Institute of Education in one programme of research found that children in nursery schools scored highest on non-verbal tests, yet their teachers spent most of their time giving verbal instructions of guidance. We must surely have teachers who could balance the approach, taking into account skills in young children

nd capabilities of the receiving child. Handling, ing, drawing, shaping and imitation of movement ary as words, and add significantly to successful of information, for instance when showing how to rs and paper, how to climb, how to tie shoelaces and mplish all the other perceptual motor skills necessary through the school day.

There are many good books on how to provide specific movement experiences for children and the development of athletics, games, gymnastics, outdoor pursuits and swimming for older pupils, so it is necessary only to point out that at every age the child may be motivated through his interest and curiosity, but the development of new skills and concepts will move fruitfully through guided exploration and structured teaching. The foundations of good movement and success in the main aspects of physical education depend on the ability to interact to information communicated and received from the environment.

Part of the information received and communicated will be essentially components of aesthetic perceptions such as form and pattern, rhythm and shape. The child who has experienced movement from this point of view is more likely to appreciate aesthetic meanings in later experiences enhancing the quality of life. The teacher's function is to provide a rich environment encouraging creative expression in a manner appropriate to his stage of development, giving particular consideration to special interests and capabilities of the individual child rather than relying on standardised expectations.

The teacher should be concerned with the information available for the child, and be aware of the balance between drawing attention to what is relevant and needs to be teased out in the development of perceptual abilities. For example, the development of abilities of scanning, hand/eye co-ordination, manipulative skill, figure/ground differentiation and spatial abilities such as measuring, positioning and judgment of distances are essential abilities required in the aspects of the movement studies curriculum. More teachers need to be aware of the experiences they are providing for the development of such abilities essential for further communicative interactions.

The setting up of complex and novel situations will test out the inventiveness and problem-solving aspects of the child as well as the provision for the intuitive and the artistic through dance and music, sport and art. For the young child movement may be the only means of expressing such knowledge, and for older children it may provide a more satisfactory way, especially in new situations.

> It is easier to recognise the variety of childhood actions than it is to understand what it is they express: yet for children in their early years movement is the only language by which they can express and communicate how they feel (Jordan, 1966).

The close relationships have been discussed earlier between movement and language, and movement and social skills. It has been suggested that the acquisition of language, perceptual-motor and social skills may be based on the same model, as shown in Figure 4.1.

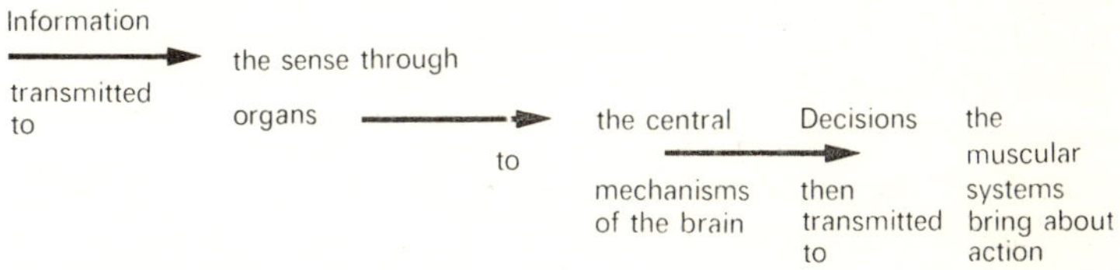

Figure 4.1

The feedback as to the appropriateness of the action then becomes part of the information transmitted to the sense organs. There is growing evidence that the interrelationships of these skills are more subtle and profound than previously suspected. Piaget (1953) for instance argued that during the early stages of life the infant knew his world only in terms of sensory impressions and motor activities. More recent research suggests that before the infant is one year old he has become a thinking creature who activates cognitive structures to resolve discrepancies and solve problems.

Programmes of physical exercises to stimulate babies to develop perceptual-motor skills earlier have been devised by Dr Jaroslav Koch at the Institute for the Care of Mother and Child in Prague. He believes that small babies have possibilities within them which may be lost if they are not developed in the first year of life. The babies following his programme of exercises have a vocabulary of up to twenty words instead of the traditional babies' five. The infant brain is still developing after birth and the type of environment the child experiences may affect the way he sees the world and responds in later life.

Research has also shown that social interactions are normally beginning in the first few months of life, and non-verbal gestures have a significant role to play in social communications between pre-school children (Blurton Jones, 1967). The precocity of social skills is related to perceptual-motor development. The child who is slower at developing perceptual-motor skills is held back. For instance, he will still be struggling to fasten buttons when the precocious child is on to his next pursuit; interacting with his teacher: taking messages, all widening his social horizons and thereby opportunities for language in different social settings, furthering social and movement skills in the orientation of himself in new physical surroundings.

The influence of such findings brought about the development of a new approach to the planning of a course of training for teachers of nursery/infant children. Instead of the movement part of the curriculum which was associated only with the understanding of music or the cathartic release of energy, the devised plan sought to furnish students with a knowledge of the sequential development of perceptual motor skill and the significance of movement in the acquisition of social and language skills in the young child.

Here is a brief outline. The course provides students with knowledge of physical development, paying particular attention to the sequential development of skill and interrelating with all the other aspects of child development. This is buttressed by the education tutor, and seen and observed in the playgroup with children of 3–5 years, and through films and reading. It attempts to provide depth of theoretical knowledge of the development of perceptual-motor skill and some of the psychological and physiological aspects of acquiring skill. This again is seen through playgroup observation but also through work in school, in which the students have been guided and in which they have planned short programmes in which they have tried out at naïve level certain tasks with a particular age group, e.g. judgment of a ball in motion, hand/eye co-ordination skills.

At the same time they are led to appreciate the multi-sensory nature of acquiring skill and encouraged through their own thinking to assess the importance of the interrelationship of visual, auditory, tactile and kinaesthetic cues.

The development of specific skills and ideas which help the child to develop abilities in ball and other apparatus handling and managing his own body in jumping, climbing, stepping and balancing activities; and to relate ideas in movement imaginatively and with other stimuli such as music, patterns, pictures, words.

Particular emphasis is on perception, as we are trying to help the student to see how and where to structure situations and to make the most of experiences arising to develop perceptual motor abilities, that is understanding of the following: Laterality/directionality. Ocular scanning. Hand/eye co-ordination. Manipulative skill. General co-ordination. Language skill development essential to understanding. Spatial abilities: measurement, positioning, distance. For the words to convey the correct meanings. Whole/part: ability to see elements in patterns or arrays and shift from whole to part. Classification: colour, size, shape, texture. Sequence: ordering, predicting. Clue awareness: ability to see and use clues in problem solving. Set together with language development. Cognitive development—children's thinking guided by other subject and education tutors.

The use of the playgroup situation is carefully controlled: contact with children is timetabled through the playgroup supervisor, and the observation panel used only by pre-arrangement of tutors and guided by outline programmes. We work with a nursery head teacher who comes in for one morning to help the students to observe or be with children in a constructive manner. On this basis of knowledge studied in depth, the factors in developing curriculum were considered. This seemed to lead the students into a more coherent and knowledgeable view of child development and the understanding to plan effectively in the educational situation. The theoretical work was supported concurrently with guided observation of young children and practical opportunities to try out ideas based on this approach. The value of logical planning for early learning was substantial, and this evidence confirmed my opinion that every teacher should be a teacher of movement studies no matter what age group he or she teaches, for the more effective learning and integration of skills required for an adaptable and richer life style.

References

Argyle, M. (1964), *The Psychology of Interpersonal Behaviour*, Harmondsworth, Penguin.

Blurton Jones, N. G. (1967), 'The Role of Non-verbal Gestures in the Social Inter-actions of Nursery School Children', in D. Morris (ed.), *Primate Ethology*, London, Weidenfeld & Nicolson.

Brooke, J. D. and Whiting, H. T. A. (eds) (1973), *Human Movement: A*

Field of Study, London, Henry Kimpton.
Condon, W. (1974), 'Speech makes Babies Move', *New Scientist*, 6 June, 624–7.
Cratty, B. J. (1964), *Movement Behavior and Motor Learning*, Philadelphia, Lea & Febiger.
Jordan, D. (1966), *Childhood and Movement*, London, Blackwell.
Laban, R. (1966), *Choreutics*, London, Macdonald & Evans.
Lamb, W. (1965), *Posture and Gesture*, London, Duckworth.
Mauldon, E. (1973), Communication through movement. In Brooke, J. D. and Whiting, H. T. A. (eds), *Human Movement: A Field of Study*, London, Henry Kimpton.
North, M. (1974), *Movement Education*, London, Maurice Temple Smith.
Phenix, P. H. (1964), *Realms of Meaning*, New York, McGraw-Hill.
Piaget, J. (1953), *The Origins of Intelligence in the Child*, New York, Basic Books.
Redfern, H. B. (1973), *Concepts in Modern Educational Dance*, London, Henry Kimpton.

5

The use of language in movement teaching

E. M. Hinks

When writing about language in relation to movement, it is necessary to state that this is only one individual's thought and approach to this important and exciting tool for the teacher. There is no single way nor universal language which is used when speaking about movement. Each speaks from his or her own beliefs and understanding or from some experience which has touched him or her individually. Nevertheless, the thoughts of the individual about the use of language in relation to the teaching of movement can be stimulated by other ideas on the subject, and it is hoped that this article may serve this purpose.

Words are symbols. They represent something and in any one context are understood to mean this. The same word in a different context may have a different meaning, and it is therefore necessary that both the speaker and the listener understand and recognise the context in which the words are being used. If this is initially accepted, then the full richness of the English language is at the service of the teacher.

Two questions need to be asked. For what purpose and in what context are the words being used? Does the meaning of words differ according to the purpose? I would suggest that this can be so, and that each teacher should search out and know for himself the meaning which is to be given to particular words, and that the group with whom he is working should also be led to understand these words in the context and purpose for which they are used. It can sometimes happen that a particular use of language is specific to one teacher and the groups with which he works.

It is my belief that how one speaks about movement affects the learning which takes place. It is, therefore, important for the teacher to select language that helps to evoke the movement response that is required. How one speaks about movement arises from how one thinks about movement. The words selected should, ideally, come out of a sound and deep knowledge of the subject, and a teacher must be free to express his meaning in his own way. Words can come to life only through the use and meaning that he gives them, in relation to his purpose and the understanding of the group.

Words used in this way create or have attached to them an image. Words can urge on, set back, or lift forward; they can ignite, kill or bring back to life; they can unlock and open up pathways, ideas, feelings and experiences. They can also close down or deprive. Words can be one of the great incentives for a class, and the manner in which they are used by the teacher is of vital importance in the promotion of learning.

From the richness of our own language one can seek words that are evocative of quality, words which add interest and often excitement to the listener. Alongside this selection of words is the necessity for the teacher to translate theoretical knowledge of his subject into the practical language which the people in his classes can understand in movement terms. For example, the use of standard technical language such as bending and stretching, meeting and parting, gathering and scattering may not be sufficient. In the practical teaching situation it may be necessary, for instance in trying to get people to achieve the feeling of stretch, to use such expressions as 'Push the part out!', 'Reach far away!'; to experience 'parting', 'Open the body out!', 'How far can you get your fingers away from your thumbs?' or 'your hips looking away from one another?'; to get a feeling of narrowness, 'Make the shoulders look at each other!' A teacher must use his imagination to find language which will give movement feeling and spark off movement effort. He must try to have at his fingertips words which will ignite the movement latent in his students. Practice and a lively mind will come to his aid in his striving to find exciting and evocative words. The following are some examples of the use of language by a movement teacher. They are examples only, and were specific to a particular situation and class.

In preparation

Enliven the body . . . is the body being *sluggardly* . . . the movement is being *reluctant* . . . make the legs *talk* . . . try not to get *grooved* into *contracted space*. . . .

In working for form

Ask your body *questions*. It will answer in *movement* not in words . . . *clear form* . . . totally *alive* with *no fading* . . . *stillness not blankness*. . . .

In working for lightness

Briskness, tautness . . . the body *bursts* into sudden action . . . a *puckish* quality . . . it collects itself up and *contains* its lightness . . . move with *audacity* into space. . . .

Descriptive words, expressive words such as 'tingle', 'sparkle', 'twinkle', words which carry the quality within them, are often helpful in lifting the learner over the brink. Language should be used constructively whenever possible. The building words rather than the negative, expressions such as 'use more of this' or 'less of this', rather than 'don't use this or that' are more helpful.

Going with the selection and use of words is the importance of the use of the voice. Without variety, flexibility and sensitivity even beautiful words can lose their meaning and power. When the words and the sound are matched together into a unit, people may be inspired to move with quality and sensitivity. Simple words, practical words, beautiful words, spoken with sincerity out of a depth of knowledge and experience, can lead to exciting movement. Words can bridge across many aspects of learning, and their magic can stimulate the mind and body to reach unexpected and often undreamed-of heights. Everyone concerned with the teaching of movement should search to find the words which illuminate movement for them. The practical language that is meaningful to them is the most likely to be meaningful to their classes.

Much of the use of language comes from the ability to observe, and observation of movement as a teaching technique needs now to be considered. Observation can be used in many ways, and the manner and outcome of the observation will depend on the purpose for which it was used. It might have been used in order to learn for oneself, to find out more about a movement activity, to record in detail, to assess and examine movement ability, or to help others to learn and achieve. It is in the latter sense that observation is used as a teaching technique.

The ability of a teacher to use his observation of movement develops as his knowledge develops and his powers of observation become more acute and refined. These two facets blend together as a result of practical experience. To strive for this is fascinating and absorbing, but it is not easy to achieve. As with the use of language, each teacher will develop his own techniques. The following thoughts on observation are set out for those interested in knowing more of the possibilities open to the teacher who has learnt to use this tool, and who would find some guiding lines helpful in developing their own skill.

If the observer structures the way he looks to the bodily heritage to move, then questions arise such as: How can the body be moved and used? How is it being used? In what ways? How widely? To what purposes? All these questions may need to be answered when looking at a group of students moving, and the asking of such questions is the beginning of the growth of the skill of movement observation for the teacher.

The observer will look according to the main purpose of the prepared lesson. It may be that the *physical* needs and abilities of the group have the main stress. The attention may be focused on the way in which the total body is being used in relation to the task set, or focused on pre-selected parts of the body. The looking may be concerned with the manner in which the space is being used by the movers, both in the use of the body as a whole and in the way in which the different parts are being placed in relation to each other. Interest in the quality of the movement may be predominant in the teacher's mind. There is no set pattern or structure to trammel the teacher's looking. Sometimes one way may be predominant, sometimes another. The choice is governed only by the needs of the group and the teacher's decision. It is only important for the teacher to know which focus has been selected, for what reason, and that for the time being all others may be ignored.

Whatever the focus, the guidelines remain the same for the looking. The teacher may look at the total body, body parts, how many parts, in what relationship, in what way; for strength in the whole or the parts. The observer may look for body line, body flow, body energy; for the clearly expressed intention of the movement, the mind of the mover knowing and his body feeling. It may be that the observer is concerned to see whether the movement would be more effective if it were smaller or larger. Is it too small, and therefore is a cramped effect seen? If it is too large then the co-ordination may be upset because the relationship between the extremities and the centre of the body is lost. Is the movement too strong or not strong enough? Is it taking place too late or too soon? Is the movement being cut off and so is incomplete and unsatisfying, or is it meandering on and to no conclusion? What is the body trying to do? From what idea does the movement spring and is the resulting movement following in a logical pathway?

Looking in another way, the observer may look for variety in the movement patterns used by the individual, for variety in the qualities used. Is there variety in both these, or is every task answered in the same manner? Observation may be of the changing shapes within the movement and of the flow of one shape into the next, or of the relevance of the movement to the achievement of the idea. Is there rhythmic content or is this absent, leaving a flat continuous phrase with no stresses or dissolving of tensions?

These suggestions are put forward as lines of thought about the use of observation as an aid to teaching. The subject is unending and only some of the areas have been touched on. The ability to observe accurately, and to be able to use one's observations in a way helpful to one's classes, comes only with practice. It must be used in a manner individual to each teacher. It needs courage and initiative but can be most rewarding. Hand in hand with the development of the ability to observe must be the gradual enrichment of the teacher's use of language, so that he is able to express his thoughts about what he sees in a way which will inspire his students.

6

Expression and communication in movement[1]

J. E. Kane

Human movement may be considered analytically from a number of viewpoints. Possibly the simplest and most useful distinction for the purpose of the behavioural analysis of human movement has been made by Allport in suggesting that every action has both a coping and an expressive dimension. The coping aspects of movement are instrumental in that they are concerned with the effective completion of a task (as in opening a door) and quantitative in that they involve measurable force (as emphasised in running, jumping and throwing). The expressive dimension of movement may be taken to refer to the quality, manner or style of performing, and is to be assessed in terms of the impact on our phenomenal awareness.

The admixture of coping and expression varies, of course, from movement to movement. In sporting activity the coping elements are paramount, but in art forms such as dance the expressive, and more comprehensively the qualitative elements predominate, and may be evaluated and analysed not so much in terms of dynamics and force, but in terms of sensory and perceptual experience. Sandle (1972) makes the important point that non-coping dimensions of movement should be considered as taking in much more than a narrow interpretation of expressive movement, and he suggests the general term 'qualitative movement', which he proposes to cover five sub-categories of which expressive movement is one. The other four are (1) self-aware movement, where the qualitative aspect emphasises the phenomenal realisation and pleasure in moving; (2) form-aware movement, where the body configuration, its symmetry, balance, proportion, pattern and unity for instance allow an interpretation of body composition or form; (3) emblematic movement, in which the movement has certain symbolic meaning for the perceiver or performer, reflective of values, attitudes and belief which give rise to stereotypic evaluation of its qualitative content, and (4) movement communication, in which the qualitative elements of an individual's movement represent the variables in the effective perception of their meaning by another.

The purpose of this paper, however, is to discuss only those two interacting and overlapping qualitative categories of movement which are concerned with expression and communication.

Expressive movement

Expressive behaviour may, according to Allport's interpretation, be considered simply as the manner or style of performing adaptive acts. Allport illustrates this general point by asking us to consider our reaction to a strange lecturer delivering his paper. While we may be most concerned with *what* he is saying and how he is coping with the topic, we are increasingly impressed at a lower level of communication with his appearance, manner and general style. Allport's hypothetical lecturer was young, neat, slender, smiled frequently, spoke rapidly in a raspy voice and scrawled illegibly on the blackboard. On the basis of these and other low-level perceptions Allport suggests that we may make inferences about the man as a person, even though these inferences are 'fleeting, fringelike and unimportant'. We may think to ourselves, 'He is insecure, self-centred but learned, humorous though cynical; on the whole I don't like him and I pity his wife' (Allport, 1961). In this kind of way we apparently draw inferences about individuals on the basis of the expressive aspects of their behaviour—their voice, facial expression, speech, posture, attitude, gesture and gait. The individual is thus revealed to us not so much by what he is doing as by the manner and style of doing it.

Expressive movement may then be considered as a means by which the individual's personality may be revealed. It may be as North (1972) suggests that 'a person uses his own wide range of movement patterns, both subtle and crude, in gesture and "shadow" movements in order to try to balance his own inner attitudes'. In the expressive movement of an angry person, for example, we may be seeing an attempt to establish inner balance—a fight with the inner emotional state. It seems likely at any rate that the expressive quality of movement emanates from the individual's feelings. The perceiver who describes a visual entity or movement as 'angry', 'sad', 'beautiful', 'strong', 'graceful', is attempting to relate these expressive qualities which he perceives to the actual emotions which he feels or has experienced.

The argument has long been debated in physical education and sports circles as to the special value in personality development of the movement experiences involved, but there are few definitive guidelines based on rigorous research. At any rate is it possible in many physical education systems (e.g. in Britain) for one to identify in the details of programmes of work statements about the inbuilt complementary 'functional' and 'expressive' concepts of movement (terms which, of course, correspond to Allport's 'coping' and 'expressive' aspects of behaviour)? It may be that the future research aimed at investigating the personality aspects of our work would do well to concentrate on the proposed expressive elements in movement. Few recent studies exist to define the nature and correlates of expressiveness in movement, though there has existed for some long time now the highly pertinent model and approach reported by Allport and Vernon in their book, *Studies in Expressive Movement*, published in 1933. Naturally our interpretation now of the term 'expressive movement' has wider and more dynamic connotations reflecting developments and elaborations in the meaning and scope of human movement in physical education and sport. Nevertheless, I am convinced that this report represents a seminal statement for those interested in the analysis and understanding of expressive movement, and I therefore propose to outline the study and comment on it. The authors undertook as a starting point a tentative classification of the many possible sources of expressiveness and suggested as a result the following six major categories:

1 general features of expressive movement which may be manifest during any activity—e.g. appearance and posture, perseverance, regularity; auxiliary movements
2 observations of standing, walking and related activities—e.g. position of hands, length of stride, speed of walk
3 observation of sitting and resting positions and the relationship of body parts to one another
4 observation of communication—e.g. attributes of voice, style

of speech, motor attitudes and gesture
5 assessment of handwriting
6 other accessible aspects of expression—e.g. art styles preferred, nicknames, games playing propensity, dress.

From this classification thirty-four variables were identified which were assessed by a number of ingeniously constructed tests and rating scales. The thirty-four tests included (a) reading and counting, (b) walking and strolling, (c) the estimation of sizes, distances, angles and weights, (d) the arranging of cubes, (e) tapping and compression of a stylus, (f) the assessment of handwriting and (g) the rating of other personal aspects of expressive movement.

On the basis of the intercorrelations between the variables the author identified three major group factors of psychological significance which they proposed to account for expressive movement. These three independent factors were named areal, centrifugal and emphasis, and the authors found that scores on the factors were reasonably constant, discriminating and distinctive so that together they could be taken to represent an accurate view of the expressive elements of personality.

The areal factor signified an expansive motor tendency, and had high loadings on spatial measurements especially of length, overall size and area. The centrifugal factor was found to be quite a separate independent spatial entity and 'outward-tendency', 'freedom' and 'extroversion' of expressive movement. The emphasis factor was found to be much more heterogeneous than the other two and emphasised physical energy with major components drawn from measures of pressure, intensity and forcefulness.

Now it must have occurred to those who have followed this brief description of the Allport/Vernon study that the factors they proposed to explain the expressive movement aspect of personality correspond in many ways to dimensions of movement which have general currency in movement studies, especially among those who follow in their teaching and interpretations the principles set down by Rudolf Laban (see North, 1972). The areal factor might seem to correspond psychologically to what Laban referred to as attitude to personal space (Kinesphere) according to which the individual tends to prefer to move idiosyncratically in a more or less expansive manner. The factor given the name centrifugal is also a spatial element indicative of movements away from the body, but is proposed also to have psychological meaning in terms of extroversion. The same notion comes through Laban's writing concerning central and peripheral movement, and the individual's attitude to the movement as expressed in the kind of effort mixture used. The centrifugal factor would clearly load highly on the Laban basic effort action which is designated 'thrusting and slashing'. The third Allport/Vernon dimension, emphasis, seems to be the clear analogy of Laban's elaborate concept of effort which embodies quantitatively eight basic combinations of his motion 'factors' weight, space, time and flow and qualitatively the mover's inner attitude or feeling towards the movement expressed as effort elements (i.e. direct–flexible, firm–fine touch, sudden–sustained, bound–free).

While these apparently major points of similarity and correspondence have been emphasised there are a number of other findings in the Allport/Vernon study that would repay careful scrutiny by those who are searching for appropriate experimental research approaches to investigate current problems in expressive movement. In general it might seem to be particularly profitable to repeat the study following a similar approach, but attempting to substitute or add variables representing more dynamic aspects of expressive movement. Modern developments in component and factor analysis would certainly permit the study to be undertaken on a larger scale so that the consistency and clarity of the dimensions explaining expressive movement might be identified. There remain, of course, the problems of observing and rating the expressive element of movement, and of producing satisfactorily high inter-observer reliabilities, though it is true that some tentative approaches have been recently undertaken and with some success. Marion North (1972) for instance has reported in detail on the development of a technique for observing and recording those aspects of movement which are particularly revealing of the personality. Unfortunately no standardised measures of personality were included in her study, so that the issue of validation has not been so far faced. A current study in London University is, however, attempting a more comprehensive approach to the problem. The study sought initially to classify the possible variables that might explain expressiveness in movement and to standardise observational and rating techniques, both of the consciously preferred forms of movement and of the unconscious 'shadow' movements. Factor analytic procedures are being utilised to identify the major explanatory dimensions, and these are then to be used in a major related study which includes a number of established objective measures of personality and related phenomena (self-image, self-concept, body-concept). It is expected that the findings will allow a more assured explanation of the underpinning dimensions of expressive movement, and the way these are linked with known personality traits and other forms of expressiveness. The critical issue in this and other similar studies is to establish reasonably objective methods of judging expressiveness in movement. Both for the perceiver and the actor there may well be semantic confusion. The word 'sad' may have, for instance, quite different movement connotations, so that it is clearly necessary for expressive qualities to be defined within an objective 'semantic space', perhaps along the lines suggested by Osgood's semantic differential. This would seem to be a serious possibility, as experienced dancers do demonstrate some consistency in their expressive movement interpretation of such notions as 'strength', 'sadness' and 'night', particularly with respect to movement criteria categorised as speed, range, shape, tension, direction and 'centre'.

Another profitable line of enquiry would be to investigate the personality trait correlates of expressive behaviour. The Allport and Vernon study indicated an extroversion dimension, and in Cattell's study of creative artists the following traits were consistently found: schizothymia (A –), intelligence (B), ego strength (C), dominance (E), desurgency (E –), low group superego standards (G –), and sensitivity (I). A serious personality study of dancers is long overdue, especially as it has been suggested that professional dancers are likely to encounter personality difficulties (Sandle, 1972).

Movement communication

The communication qualities and values of movement are in many ways to be seen as overlapping with expressive qualities, so that what a person communicates is often considered to be what he expresses. However, it is the social context within which an expressive movement occurs that gives it its special communication value.

In the area of developmental psychology there has always been a generous acknowledgment of the importance of movement communication for children in so far as movement, certainly for the pre-operational child, may be more than an aid to language when the child wishes to express and communicate what he feels. It is agreed by Bruner that language development and a child's experience and understanding operate independently for a long time so that a 'mismatch' often exists between what is said and what is felt and understood. Some London University studies, as well as others, are now proceeding to assess the contribution that related movement experiences may have in reducing this mismatching or incongruence by broadening and elaborating the understanding of semantic terms through appropriate movement experiences.

The way in which intentional and unintentional expressive movements affect interpersonal relationships has become of increased interest and meaning in movement studies. Goffman (1971) considers such expressive acts to be the basis of an information game played by the 'actor' and perceiver in which the actor's verbal and non-verbal cues are intentionally 'given out' or unintentionally 'given off' (cf. Laban's 'shadow' movements) and monitored for credibility. The term kinesics has been given to this sort of non-verbal communication which is described as 'the systematic study of how human beings communicate through body movement or gesture'. A number of investigators have explored the ways in which different parts of the body are used in non-verbal communication and it appears that the eyes, face and head cues in general are more informative about the nature of emotions and feelings, and are the vital sources of social techniques, while the body is the main indicator of intensity of emotions. The face has apparently not only the greatest sending capacity, but is also the major non-verbal liar during efforts at deception (Ekman and Friesen, 1969). The implication of non-verbal sources of communication for dance and movement drama seems obvious since the expressive qualities must normally relate to intended mood and emotion of the role, and also may need to relate to the expressive qualities of others. In sport, too, the interpretation of movement cues is important, especially in two-man competitive confrontations. The way in which different parts of the body function as a communicating system, both unintentionally and intentionally with a view to deceiving an opponent has recently been investigated, with the findings giving confirmation of the proposal that opponents are more likely to be deceived by head and upper body movements. The term meta-incongruence has been proposed to describe those situations where the body movement and the accompanying verbal statement are at variance, as is often the case with insincere social interactions as in 'How nice to see you' being accompanied by a perfunctory glance and a flabby handshake. There is also the most interesting suggestion from Birdwhistell (1960) for the existence of kinesic leaders who presumably attain their position of status and authority not so much as a result of their verbal contribution, but by virtue of the impelling communication force of their movements. No doubt in dance the opportunities for kinesic leaders to emerge are many, but one can only speculate on the usefulness of considering in the context of team sport, and especially team leadership, the value of taking into account individuals' kinesic power.

Elaborating the notions of kinesics are those of proxemics or territoriality which, for the purposes of human movement studies, centres on the importance of personal space, and how it is consciously or unconsciously structured. In a sense personal space may be seen as a linked extension of the body boundary which encompasses a sector of space that is uniquely one's own, and which represents the centre and base of operations in the world, the outward projection as it were of one's inner being and identity. Personal space is proposed to take in the variable near space beyond the body boundary on which the individual lays special claim, and which is highly guarded against intrusion so that others who are willingly allowed to share it are specially privileged. There are apparently social status, cultural and sex determinants of the amount and shape of personal space available to the individual. With respect to cultural differences, reference has been made by Argyle (1967) to the problems reported at international meetings at which Americans and Europeans have been seen steadily retreating backwards or gyrating in circles to preserve their personal space, hotly pursued by Latin Americans trying to establish their habitual degree of proximity for inter-personal communication. The spatial demands directly in front of the face are considerably larger than at the back and sides, so that the contour of personal space tends to be regarded as egg-shaped, with the individual situated at the sharper end.

The psychological importance to the individual of his personal space and the consequences to him of its violation by encroachment or obtrusion are matters that deserve consideration in movement studies. While the shape and amount of personal space may have cultural, sex and situational determinants, they may also be linked with personality, so that constraints which militate against personal preference may affect both coping and expressive forms of behaviour. In group dance, for instance, a task and theme requiring the entering of personal space (especially if touching is involved) and the use of additional space (Goffman, 1971) that an individual may expect to have available, may need to be considered by a sensitive choreographer in terms of the inhibition and general psychological stability of the dancer. Competitive team game situations may also throw up issues where considerations of personal space are helpful. Experience and observation suggest that 'close marking' may have a deleterious effect on the performance of some athletes due mainly to the uncomfortable and harassing feelings associated with the invasion of personal space which in turn may be the cause of psychological distraction giving rise to ineffective functioning. It may be worth observing as a postscript that the area of movement studies incorporating sports, dance and a wide variety of physical activities is rich with situations suitable for the behavioural scientist in which territorial and personal space imperatives and the access to them are in question. Our field of endeavour ought, therefore, to be highly attractive to researchers interested in proxemics.

Concluding remarks

This short paper has attempted to consider the vehicle of movement for expression and communication. It would seem that body movement of a more or less dynamic form may intentionally or unintentionally reveal such qualities and in doing so pose questions about their psychological significance. There are some indications that movement expression is an important indicator of personality with which movement communication may also be linked, but little rigorous research support exists to substantiate these contentions. There is, however, experimental evidence to indicate that personal equations or preference in movement exist even though the evidence is based on relatively non-dynamic laboratory tests of personal rhythms, preferred speed, spatial preference and task persistence (Cratty, 1967). If indeed there are consistent inbuilt personal equations in the dynamic whole-body movements with which physical education, dance and sport are concerned, and if these preferences represent a projection of personality, then the challenge to investigate the dynamics of these aspects of qualitative movement is very pressing.

Note

This is a revised text of a paper given at the Third World Congress of the International Society of Sports Psychology, Madrid, 1973.

References

Allport, G. W. (1961), *Pattern and Growth in Personality*, Holt, Rinehart & Winston, New York.

Allport, G. W. and Vernon, P. E. (1933), *Studies in Expressive Movement*, Hafner, London.

Argyle, M. (1967), *The Psychology of Interpersonal Behaviour*, Penguin, Harmondsworth.

Birdwhistell, R. (1960), 'Kinesics and Communication', in E. Carpenter and M. McLuhan (eds), *Explorations in Communication*, Beacon Press, Boston.

Cratty, B. J. (1967), *Movement Behavior and Motor Learning*, Lea & Febiger, Philadelphia.

Ekman, P. and Friesen, W. V. (1969), 'Head and Body Cues in the Judgement of Emotion; a Re-formulation', *Perceptual and Motor Skills*, 24.

Goffman, E. (1971), *Relations in Public*, Penguin, Harmondsworth.

North, Marion (1972), *Personality Assessment through Movement*, Macdonald & Evans, London.

Sandle, Douglas (1972), 'Aesthetics and the Psychology of Qualitative Movement', in J. E. Kane (ed.), *Psychological Aspects of Physical Education and Sport*, Routledge & Kegan Paul, London.

7

Dance education

M. North

Our modern culture in the West does not rate the arts of movement very highly. Theatre dance, 'concert' dance, is savoured by the few—even classical ballet, which can attract the largest audiences, has to struggle to survive, and the 'modern' dance or mime artists command small audiences when compared with our cultural acceptance of, say, music. Now there are many reasons for this, but without doubt, modern man's tendency to be unaware of his body and his inability to use it and tune it to serve him—to serve his mental, emotional, social, even spiritual needs as a human being—makes him unappreciative of the art which uses the body as its instrument. It is as if he does not 'live inside' his body at all. It is interesting however that young people are now flocking to Dance Theatre, and demands for dance classes and courses are increasing. Even universities are beginning to recognise the significance of dance to the community.

The general criteria for these movement art forms do not differ from those of any art, and in trying to foresee future developments, it is apparent that the same problems and opportunities exist in dance as they do for music and drama and painting and sculpture. It is worth looking at our heritage of dance before looking forward. Many writers have expounded on the significance to human development and culture of the arts generally and dance in particular. But why should we look to the past in order to understand the present or the future? Dr Winnicott (1974) in his paper on 'Location of Cultural Experiences' suggests that cultural development always arises out of the traditions of the past in relation to the present needs—and later I wish to draw attention to the idea of the influence of the future on the present. I think that no one would deny that the level of culture in any society is assessed principally by the state of health of the arts. It is, however, often the artist who leads the society, as well as responding to its frustrations, demands and opportunities. So I shall turn first to a leading dancer and choreographer himself to say how he envisages the future and the past.

Alwin Nikolais who is the American pioneer of multi-media modern dance, says (in a BBC broadcast) 'Multi media is not the final thing—no "way" ever is. It doesn't matter what form dance takes in the future. Beauty will never die—we need beauty for ever and ever—not only that which is old, but wherever we can get it—we must certainly cherish it. I would deplore anyone who was such a faddist to think we must destroy the things of beauty because they happen not to be necessarily the thing of the moment.' It seems to me that Nikolais is totally conscious of his place in the time-stream of human development—often working as he does more in the future than in the 'thing of the moment'—always acutely aware of his past heritage.

If we attempt to tune in to our heritage of dance, we have two ways in which we can approach the task. One is to refer to recorded dances of the past, the other is to study those few remaining cultures where dance still plays an important part in society. These historical and anthropological studies are comparable with those involved in the study of music, which also, unlike paintings, buildings, carvings and even, to some extent, stories, plays, myths and poems, have survived in their original forms, through colour on canvas, carving in stone, words on paper or blocks. Musicians learned early that to record their sounds they needed a system of notation—not a precise instrument, for we cannot actually hear the sound retained, but accurate enough for the sound to be reproduced. Because of this universally accepted notation, music has prospered, developed and grown, for every human being needing to make a new music has access to his musical heritage.

Dance did not fare so well, and it is only in this century that a more or less universally acceptable notation was devised by Rudolf Laban. There are many systems used to record movement patterns, and we know of attempts at least from the tenth or eleventh century to find a comprehensive system. Now that we have such a method at last, let us have the confidence to hope that in another century it cannot be said, as Margaret D'Houbler (1962) said: 'Although dance is older, how young and neglected it seems when compared to the maturity and expansion of music.' The direct knowledge of the content of dance in the past—that is, its precise rhythms, body gestures and attitudes, its patterns, forms and changing groups—can rarely be discerned from the few verbal descriptions which we have, or the inadequate notations. Historically then, we are left with a greater understanding of the role of dance in societies than with the exact movement symbolism.

But we have been saved to some degree by a small and dedicated group of American research workers. The inspiration for a large-scale research project in 'cantometrics' came from the musicologist Alan Lomax (1968). He and his colleagues collected examples of song styles throughout the world, divided into eight world culture regions.

Remarkable distinctions in musical form and style were revealed between these areas, and later it was decided to make a comparable study of dance styles. In the report 'Dance Style and Culture' Alan Lomax, Irmgard Bartenieff and Forrestine Pauley say

> First, we wished to confirm our impression that the style areas and sets found in the analysis of singing style would be confirmed by a similar analysis of another form of expressive activity—similar patterns in dance and song. In this way an important working hypothesis of communication studies would be supported: that analogous patterns will be found at the same level in different communication systems.

(This was first proposed by Birdwhistell in 1968.) 'Birdwhistell pointed out that both music and song are derived and not primary communication systems. . . .' 'Every known culture has some form of highly redundant physical activity recognisable as dance.' (Later I come back to this expression 'highly redundant'.) It occurred to Lomax that the rhythmic or metrical aspects of song might be derived from dance and that the preferred metres in song are transferred from the most common metrical patterns of the dance. Song can then be defined as 'danced speech'. 'Therefore, if one seeks to evoke the significance of musical meter, one must turn from song to the study of the rhythmic ordering of physical activity in dance.' They further state: 'dance is considered first as a representation and reinforcement of cultural pattern and only secondarily as an expression of individual emotion.'

The report of these initial investigations into dance patterns and styles is illuminating beyond anything we have previously inferred or recorded, and the 'pay off' for our studies is enormously appreciated. Here we have an indication at last of how to recover some at least of our dance heritage, and the training of movement and dance specialists to continue to expand this work must rate as a high priority for our future work. More and more anthropologists from different schools are becoming interested in dance studies, and our MA programme in dance and education incorporates not only dance history but also dance anthropology.

I want now to discuss at what stage dance or song or painting becomes an 'art form' as distinct from a system of communication, or a magical device. Only if functional or 'useful' (in a practical sense) criteria are used can the expression quoted above, 'redundant physical activity', be appropriately used in discussing dance. It is redundant only to external practicality—and is in fact highly relevant to personal inner, and often social needs. As Lomax used the term, he means that these elements of dance (for example, gestures, postures, movement qualities, etc.) are characteristic and essential to everyday activities,

> and thus crucial to cultural continuity. By treating these elements as redundantly and formally, dance becomes an effective organiser of joint motor activity. . . . Dance captures, regulates, or orders the energy and attention of groups of people, and thereby acquires the weight of general community approval. Thus dance functions to establish and renew consensus at moments when a society, without further discussion or explanation, is ready to act in concert.

This is one view of dance and how it relates to life experiences—that is, it serves to perpetuate the social structures and ensure the continuity of the group. It seems that Lomax's main premise is that man is moulded by his environment, and society finds systems which train and direct the young into its desired plans. In this view, the dance perpetuates what is there. There are other views which deal with a more dynamic approach towards the role of the arts in society—for example, that the arts are significant in the play between society and personal influence on it. For instance, it is suggested that society builds upon innate systems in man, each kind of society selecting (a) particular area(s) which it then develops and perpetuates. It is necessary to see how culture deals with these systems, selects and builds on them. The facts about the distribution of dance styles and patterns, and their relationships with other artistic expressions, give us material with which we can begin to understand more.

Change, development and new states of consciousness are unlikely to result from a stabilised social situation. Only when pressures become unbearable, when consensus of opinion cannot be reached, when change within the ritual is 'allowed' is there sufficient motivation for development and a new focus. These pressures are always signals in an individual or a society for the possibility of a new increase of consciousness. Then an artist will attempt to make intelligible that which lies within the realm of possibilities, but for which there is yet no form, through the medium he knows best—by making a dance, a painting, a poem or song (see later example of Picasso). Hence, although his personal experience provides both motivation and content, in giving form to it he is no longer 'self expressive', making a personal statement of personal feeling, but he makes a leap beyond this to the universal symbolic statement—that is, what is a possibility for every man and later, given appropriate conditions, may become an actuality.

Professor Bantock says 'All art is concerned with feeling—personal involvement—life experience—transformed into a new statement, organised and formulated.' Experience does involve past living, past involvements in growth and strivings—but much less is it recognised that in order to understand what a present 'experience' is, we must take into account also that to which the future draws us, its influence over us and our intentions towards it. Just as there is inherent in any cell, given sufficient support from its environment, the capacity for future development within its appropriate organism, so our life actions are influenced by our innate capacities for growth and refinement of consciousness and new awareness. The artist deals with possibilities which are at that moment beyond man's present psychological and social consciousness. He does not deal with actualities. He deals with what lies ahead and beyond, and is both pulled and pulls towards the increasing growth of consciousness in the future. These innate capacities for growth of consciousness pull us towards a future more forcefully perhaps than past achievements push us towards it. Our understanding of creative processes and the making of works of art remains limited while we focus only on the past. To see dance as a force for social stability is, therefore, one view, holding us to the past—but to recognise it as a medium through which man and society can bring about change, and take hold of new consciousness through the individual's capacity for change, is another view. I am not a biologist or physicist and I can only just begin to understand generally some of the new thinking in these areas. But the language which emerges is a language of movement, and must strike chords in all movement and dance students, even though the particular applications might be obscure. In contemplating new directions in our own field, it seems helpful to understand some of these contemporary ways of thinking. M. D. Marshak discusses this whole intricate process of creativity and its relationship to art and science in 'Art Education in Relation to Psychic and Mental Functioning'.

I can only here give three short quotations which say more clearly, and extend, what I have said above. The first is from a quotation she gives from Zervos, who is talking about Picasso:

> He sees descending upon him a superior order of exigencies; he has a very clear impression that something compels him imperiously to empty his spirit of all that he has only just discovered, even before he has been able to control it, so that he can admit other suggestions. Hence his torturing doubts. But this anguish is not a misfortune for Picasso; it is just that which enables him to break down all his barriers, having the field of the possible freed to him, and opening him up to the perspectives of the unknown.

The second is from her description of the creative process:

> The act of wrenching away an object or concept from its habitual associative context and seeing it in a new context is an essential part of the creative process.
> It is an act of both destruction and creation, for it demands the breaking up of a mental habit and melting down with the blow-lamp of Artesian doubt the frozen structure of accepted theory to enable the new fusion to take place.

And the third one, which links us to the physicist:

> The attempt to locate the source of creative energy—in some past events, for example—reminds one of the advances in physical theory over the last two centuries to find the 'ultimate' and 'irreducible' primary qualities of the world. Each of these advances in physical theory with its rich technological harvest

was bought by a loss of intelligibility. Compared with the modern physicist's picture of the world, the Ptolemaic universe of epicycles and crystal spheres was a model of sanity.

Let us take the example of a single particle which is contained in a box whose base represents zero energy and whose walls represent increasing potential energy. If the particle has insufficient kinetic energy to overcome the potential energy barrier of the walls it can still be predicted with confidence that at some time the particle will appear outside the walls of the box, i.e. it will pass through what appears to be an impenetrable barrier. The point about this is that any electron—which is both a particle and a wave—to accomplish the above feat must in fact make a 'jump' which means that it dematerializes and rematerializes outside the box; that is, it does not pass through space and time. The phenomenon is known as 'quantum-mechanics tunnelling'.

To move back to our own art form, many of us feel it is important to be able to say something about the art forms of movement in which we work. Just as those who can discuss art with any penetration find it necessary to take part to whatever degree of ability they have in their art, so it is essential both to experience the art and to think about it, not simultaneously but in a series of 'oscillations between experience and thinking about it' (Marshak). This idea of oscillations between contrasting movements is as familiar to the dancer as it is to the physicist, biologist—or thinker. Creative work comes out of experience and is not valid without it, but the ability to think about the experience raises it to a conscious level, and increases personal mastery. Art experience is the most direct knowledge we can achieve. The symbol does not direct our attention away from the symbol to practical life, but as Arnaud Reid says,

> It draws meanings from life and things into itself—things as loved, hated, marvelled at, enjoyed, felt with sense of tragedy, comedy, disturbance, peace, dynamic portent . . . an infinitely variegated world of values, personally felt, but transformed in embodiment into untranslatable new meanings which must be known intuitively in aesthetic experience or not at all.

Yet in our technical age such a view is not popular, for we tend to recognise as 'true' only that which can be verified by the senses. It is ironical that while most of our lives are affected and influenced by other than these 'external' truths, we cling to rationality and literal explanations—as Jung said, 'The idea that anything can be true which does not come from outside has hardly yet dawned on mankind.' Perhaps we are moving nearer to this realisation, as the reports from physicists and biologists seem to imply—and in envisaging new directions for the arts we make a claim to a future which give regards to truths of a subtler and more 'human' kind. David McKittrick in his book *Dance* gives three pertinent quotations which I borrow here. F. W. Schilling says, 'It is not with things that man has to do in the mythological process, it is powers arising within consciousness itself that move him', and Herbert Read, talking of the existence of space as a mystery in the human consciousness, says, 'space was a nothingness out of which all imaginable powers could emerge. Some of these powers might be beneficial, others destructive, but all alike had to be propitiated. The work of art became an act of containment and propitiation.' Langer (1953) sees powers more specifically as the primary creation of dance. In *Feeling and Form* she writes: 'The dance creates an image of nameless and even bodiless Powers filling a complete autonomous realm, a "world", it is the first presentation of the world as a realm of mystic forces.'

In giving value to art forms (including dance) which structure and 'hold' these forces, which consciously or unconsciously influence us, there is a hope for future humanity. The educative justification lies in the whole creative process just as much as in the end product of an artifact.

In a practical sense, then, the future directions in the arts of movement, particularly dance, lie primarily in the development of the appreciation of the value of art itself. In order to see this development come about our teachers, producers and performers must aim not only for meaning, but also for the clarity of form in which the meaning is carried, i.e. dance craftsmanship, which is often undervalued (particularly in teaching children in this country) along with most human crafts, must be restored to respectability. Professor Peters says 'creativity without expertise is cant'.

These crafts involve the skill and precision of movement (technique), ability to write down and read movement notation, ability to use language not only to justify the inclusion of the arts in society but to help clarify and develop and communicate, and the persistency to question, investigate, discuss and research into all areas of human life which involve movement. Only in these ways shall we develop the kind of mastery of movement which is necessary for dance.

I belong to the group of people who believe that there is a body of knowledge about human movement which is the core of this particular medium of art. This body of knowledge can be conveyed to others by the most direct medium of the dance itself—the direct experience—the direct knowledge.

I do not wish to say much about the actual methods of teaching movement and dance which can be employed within the formal educational system—or indeed in society generally—except to resist the implied wholesale swing from 'closed' to 'open' attitudes as suggested by Professor Hoyle. He referred to the general swing from structured situations to freer ones; closed spaces to open plan, etc. No art can flourish in an extreme permissive atmosphere, for art requires discipline of a rigorous kind (and by rigorous, this does not mean inhuman or cruel).

Already mentioned as aids to research and records are notation systems, and films (as used in the Lomax work, and in my own child development research). These are comparable with musical scores and tapes or records. It is crucial that they be given appropriate storage and accessibility for students. In the short term, we need many more small-scale projects covering all areas of movement study and dance, well reported and available for others to study. Above all, we need the creative enthusiasms of experts working alone or in small or large teams, willing to share their findings, their strivings, their hopes and achievements, whether this is in teaching, performing, treating patients or launching new courses. I believe we are past not only our infancy but our childhood, and see the future as a struggle to launch our work into the community—academic as well as social—so that it reclaims its rightful place in equality beside the visual, musical and dramatic arts.

References

Bantock, G. H. (1967), *Education, Culture and the Emotions*, Bloomington, Indiana University Press.

D'Houbler, M. (1962), *Dance, A Creative Art Experience*, Madison, University of Wisconsin Press.

Langer, S. K. (1953), *Feeling and Form*, London, Routledge & Kegan Paul.

Lomax, A. (1968), *Folk Song, Style and Culture*, American Association for Advancement of Science (Publication 88), Washington, D.C.
McKittrick, D. (1973), *Dance*, Basingstoke, Macmillan.
Read, H. (1955), *Icon and Idea*, London, Faber & Faber.
Winnicott, D. W. (1974), *Playing and Reality*, Harmondsworth, Penguin.

Part 3

Application of scientific knowledge

8

The implications on movement studies of recent advances in biomechanics

A. J. Smith

The nature of biomechanics

Biomechanics is a multi-disciplinary approach to the study of human movement in which relevant areas of well-established disciplines are called upon to form the basis of the new field of study. Medicine, engineering and physics provide major contributions while special technologies, such as electronic instrumentation and numerical data-processing are recruited to assist with specific problems. It is not possible to give a hard-and-fast definition of the scope of biomechanics because there are several areas of development and each area is still very much in the formative stage. For the specialist in physical education a glance through the pages of the *Journal of Biomechanics* will provide very little that is of interest and, in all probability, a good deal that is totally unintelligible. The *Journal* gives weight to advanced mathematical treatments, such as stress analysis of the spinal column, fluid dynamics of blood flow and astronautical manoeuvres in the weightless state. The *Journal of Biomechanics* and other similar publications reflect the great amount of research which is going on in biomedical engineering, and here the emphasis is mainly on the analysis of internal human functions by means of engineering principles.

The study of human movement means, for the physical educationist, the study, not of internal processes, but of whole-body action, and the mechanical ideas involved are rather different from those called upon in medical biomechanics. In the present context, therefore, biomechanics may be thought of as the application of mechanical principles and mathematical techniques to the investigation of whole-body action. The interest lies mainly in understanding how the human body is propelled and how it acts upon bodies outside itself. Some aspects of co-ordination and control of human action may be studied by detailed observation of movement patterns and by computations derived therefrom. This is not to say that in movement study we have no concern with internal actions of muscles and joints within the body. Mechanical principles may, to a limited extent, be applied to the calculation of loads on muscles and joints, but such applications are likely to be used only to indicate the order of magnitude of internal body forces, rather than for precise estimation.

The multi-disciplinary nature of biomechanics does not imply that it is a conglomeration of related ideas; its ground structure is formed by the laws of mechanics, and from them explanations and predictions of human motion are derived. Indeed, it is reasonable to regard all the other contributory areas of knowledge, anatomy, physiology, and so on, as 'service' disciplines. They provide specialised techniques and invaluable data, but the working principles are those of mechanics, and they may be briefly summarised as follows:

(a) The rules concerning the action of forces on bodies and the motion produced by them.
(b) The rules dealing with the flow of work and energy into and out of a system.

Despite their apparent simplicity these principles lead to extensive developments, and there is a clear need to select with care those aspects and consequences of the laws of mechanics which are relevant to biomechanical study.

Sources of information

Several well-known contributors to the literature of biomechanics have adopted a mainly non-mathematical approach. Tricker and Tricker (17), Dyson (4) and Hopper (8) have provided valuable texts with examples and explanations of many forms of human activity. They illustrate mechanical ideas through experiments and analogies, and their work is generally regarded as prescribed reading in biomechanics. It is arguable whether, for the present purposes of physical education, there is any need to advance beyond this kind of descriptive approach to the subject. Certainly a good deal of insight into the mechanics of locomotion and athletic activity may be gained through clear diagrams and a good verbal exposition of theoretical concepts. In the author's opinion, however, some mathematical ability is essential to the proper understanding of the principles of mechanics. We should consider not only the immediate needs of the physical education course, but the provision of good fundamentals on which the student may base his later reading of more advanced work.

The step from descriptive biomechanics to even the simplest mathematical expression of basic ideas is a difficult but important one. It represents a considerable barrier for most students of physical education, for once the equations of motion are employed it is necessary to build up understanding of the rules of algebra, facility in the inter-conversion of various systems of units of measurement, and accuracy in numerical computation. Nevertheless the effort is worth making, even if much of it must be reserved for specialised post-experience courses. With good mechanical foundations it is possible to undertake useful experimental project work, such as the analysis of cine film of human motion. In addition most research papers in biomechanics call for some mathematical understanding if they are to be properly appreciated and critically assessed. The question is, how best can the student acquire the necessary background without becoming entangled in a web of mathematical complexities?

Some recent texts have helped to provide the answer by dealing with biomechanical aspects of sport in mathematical terms, the standard required being somewhere between 'O' and 'A' level. Hay (7), Daish (3), Miller and Nelson (12) and Plagenhoef (14) have produced books which are now becoming known in physical education circles and will, no doubt, be increasingly used at BEd level and beyond as working texts. The reader who wishes to make the best use of this material, but finds his mathematical knowledge falls short, is probably well advised to attend evening classes to take him to the standard of first-year 'A' level applied mathematics. There are, of course, many excellent textbooks on elementary mechanics, but they are aimed either at the potential engineer or the physicist. At present there exists a need for a basic text which takes its examples from the motion of the human body rather than of inanimate objects, but until its appearance such excellent works as French's *Newtonian Mechanics* (5) will assist greatly in private study.

Research papers in biomechanics appear in a wide range of journals. There have also been international seminars in biomechanics in Zürich, Eindhoven, Rome and Pennsylvania, whose proceedings have been published in full. Astronautics research programmes in the USA have provided many important contributions to the literature, though it is easier to obtain these papers on microfilm than in printed form. Some details of these sources are given at the end of the chapter.

The relevance of published material depends, of course, upon the interests of the reader, but the following selection of titles may indicate the scope of recent work:

'Human self-rotation by means of limb movements.'
'Computer simulation in springboard diving.'
'Some dynamic response characteristics of weightless man.'
'Forces transmitted by joints in the human body.'
'Muscular control of landing from unexpected falls.'
'The biomechanical study of gymnastic movements.'
'Elastic bounce of the body.'
'Mechanical work in running.'
'Determination of acceleration from displacement-time data.'
'A mathematical model of the human body.'

The excellence of much research material must be emphasised, but at the same time it is unwise to accept all published work without question. In the current vogue for publication papers sometimes appear without sufficient thought having been given to their mathematical foundations, and incorrect statements in mechanics have formed the basis of detailed research. This only serves to underline the need for good basic teaching in biomechanics.

Introductory work in biomechanics

Despite the multi-disciplinary nature of the subject, a first course in biomechanics should avoid a multi-disciplinary approach. By this we imply that if a student is given a smattering of anatomy, mechanics, electromyography and so on, he will have much difficulty in interrelating such varied information, relevant though it all is to his interests. If on the other hand he can acquire a 'feel' for the fundamentals of mechanics, which describe the motion and functioning of many types of system, he may later go on to see that many of the other disciplines in biomechanics serve to provide data for the equations of motion.

Mechanical principles also provide links between biomechanics and other areas of movement study. The visco-elastic models of muscle action are mechanical interpretations based on combinations of springs, viscous resistances and contractile elements; many standard experiments in exercise physiology are based on the work–energy principle; and the study of psychological aspects of skill employs the concept of feedback control, widely applied to mechanical systems.

The necessary 'feel' for mechanical ideas cannot be achieved by textbook study and paper work. Simple experiments to illustrate each step of the development are essential, and there is much scope for inventiveness in this sphere. Some of the descriptive texts in biomechanics, cited above, suggest experiments in which the student is a force-producing and force-sensing participant. The experience, for example, of hauling a sizeable load up an incline, with and without acceleration, can bring home a fundamental point in a way which cannot be matched by reading or explanation. There is room here to exploit the physical education student's natural interest in physical activity, and we should not forget that for centuries man's knowledge of force and motion came from his experience of manual labour. The bodily 'feel' of lifting, pulling and pushing led him to devise ways of reducing physical effort. He learnt to combine the efforts of several men and then to rig up simple devices which became the first labour-saving machines. A worthwhile teaching programme might well be based on the history of mechanics.

Alongside these kinds of experiment there must be a parallel development of basic theory and simple calculation. Here seems to be one of the main problems in a movement study course, and some suggestions have already been made for tackling it. Even leaving aside biomechanics, there is a certain imbalance in teaching if the student has detailed understanding of the physiological processes involved in the cycle ergometer test, but cannot calculate the horsepower produced, given the pedalling speed and the brake load. One of his difficulties in performing the calculation will be in the conversion of units, from the 'Kilopond' beloved by cycle ergometer manufacturers to the 'British' system of force measurement. The units problem will be with us for many years to come, for despite the universal acceptance of the metric Système

Internationale (SI), many important earlier publications will remain in print with a variety of metric, 'British' and 'absolute' systems of units built into them.

One further point on fundamentals should be made, and that concerns definitions. Definitions clarify concepts, and time spent on them is always valuable. The mere repetition of a sentence—'power equals force times velocity', for instance—is but the beginning of wisdom. The statement is a limited definition of 'power', satisfactory provided one can show, in a given situation, which force and velocity are to be multiplied, and more significantly, provided one understands that the multiplication together of certain forces and velocities gives a totally meaningless result. 'Power' must be discussed and illustrated at some length before a proper appreciation of the concept is achieved. Along the way more colloquial uses of the word 'power', in athletics and in everyday life, must be disposed of. Is so much debate on a single word really worth while? Perhaps so, when at least two biomechanical papers in accredited journals have been based on misconceptions of the idea of power.

Experimental techniques

A perusal of research literature will show that a relatively small number of experimental techniques are employed in the majority of biomechanical studies. These established methods are becoming the bread-and-butter methods of biomechanics, and refinements are taking place all the while.

Cine-filming is favoured as a method of motion recording because little impediment is offered to the subject's movement. Recently three-dimensional motion analysis has been carried out using two, or sometimes three, synchronised cameras.

Single-plate camera shots, in which multiple images of the movement appear on the same picture, may be produced by stroboscopy or by a rotating-disc shutter. The attractive results obtained are perhaps of more value as visual aids than as serious research material.

Electromyography is still widely used as an indicator of muscular activity and sometimes it is proposed as a quantitative measure of muscular tension. The current view of leading authorities seems to be that the use of e.m.g. to measure tension is seldom justified, and such claims must be viewed with caution.

A force plate is, in effect, an extremely rigid and sensitive weighing machine. The most useful form is a rectangular plate let into a smooth floor, with no appreciable gaps or steps at the edges, so that the performer may freely walk, run or jump on and off the plate. As he makes contact sensitive pick-ups beneath the plate measure the variations in thrust. These force variations are recorded, and may be related to other features of the movement pattern. To this end filming and electromyography are often carried out simultaneously with force-plate measurements.

Most force plates have been laboratory built, but at least one version is now available commercially (11). Most of these devices are expensive. A moderately priced version for teaching and simple experiments is much needed, and some moves have been made in this direction (15).

Alongside these well-tried techniques new methods of instrumentation are being developed. Three examples may illustrate the range of application:

(a) In reading movement data from cine film of human activity it is usual to project each frame of the film on to a screen and measure the co-ordinates of each hinge point (knee, elbow, etc.). This is a laborious task if the readings are taken 'by hand', but a recently reported semi-automatic scanning device (10) removes much of the drudgery and the possibility of human error. The scanner is 'on-line' to a computer and transmits hinge-point co-ordinates directly as data for biomechanical analysis.

(b) In addition to electromyography it has recently been proposed that small muscle sounds during contraction may also be picked up and recorded as an indication of the magnitude of muscular activity. The technique may have advantages over electromyography in operational simplicity (1).

(c) Angular motion of body segments, particularly of the upper and lower leg, has been used in the analysis of walking and running patterns (6). The angles may be measured frame-by-frame on the cine film, but a new technique renders both the taking of the film and the lengthy process of measurement unnecessary. Using photo-electric sensors mounted on the limb, and a polarised rotating light beam, the device produces a record of angular variations during motion (13).

The development of these techniques, (a) by an engineering research centre, (b) by a department of physiology and (c) independently by a medical biomechanics unit and an institute of ergonomics, emphasises once more the multi-disciplinary character of biomechanics and its dependence on specialists in many fields.

Mathematical analysis and computer methods

Mathematical analysis of a mechanics problem passes through two distinct stages. The first stage is the setting up of the equations which specify the system in question and its behaviour—a mathematical model. In the case of human motion the mathematical model often employs a segmental representation of the body, that is, one in which the body is thought of as a system of interconnected masses; the connections are the main skeletal joints and the masses simulate the segments—thigh, forearm and so on.

The second stage is the solution of the working equations, and two paths are open here. Either the analysis may be pushed through in mathematical form, using perhaps techniques of algebra and the calculus; or the equations may be written into a computer program—'computer modelling'—together with the necessary data, and solutions achieved by purely numerical operations controlled by the working equations in the program. With smaller problems the numerical work may be carried out on a desk calculator.

Good examples of both methods, the analytical and the numerical, have appeared in recent literature (9, 14). Analytical solutions give much insight into the mechanical processes taking place, but the mathematics may quickly become very difficult or impossible. The numerical approach on the computer offers a more versatile approach. Numerical data may be fed directly to the computer from measuring instruments by 'on-line' computing; variation of a specific factor in the problem may often be investigated by changing a few lines in the program; and the output from the computer may be in the form of graphs and diagrams of body action printed on paper or displayed on a screen by 'computer graphics'. These and other advantages of computer methods are available only when a suitable program has been written and tested. However, some biomechanical computer programs have been published and others are in course of development (2, 14, 16).

Biomedical engineering

Liaisons between medicine and engineering have given rise to many advances in the field of artificial limbs and replacements for human joints. Although much of this work is essentially of medical interest, the fundamental studies of the pattern of locomotion and the bones which are borne by ligaments, joints and muscles are of general interest in biomechanics. In such studies the internal body actions must be 'modelled' by a somewhat simplified mechanical representation before mathematical analysis can be carried out. These investigations have made it necessary to obtain reasonably accurate anatomical dimensions of joints and muscle locations (14) and to develop new methods of instrumentation (1, 13). Attempts have also been made to assess some of the mechanical causes of sports injury (14, 16).

Conclusion

This sketch of recent work cannot do justice to the many facets of biomechanics. It may, however, indicate that an approach to the subject through a survey of the varied experimental techniques will not provide a systematic framework for study. If we are to put the study of biomechanics on a par with undergraduate work in physics or engineering we shall do well to learn from those older disciplines. Although a student may be drawn to physics through the mysteries of astronomy, or to engineering through the fascination of aeronautics, he will spend much of his time on basic theory and experiment which seem a far cry from his initial interests. None the less the procedure has been proved a sound one, and we shall be unwise to ignore it in the teaching of biomechanics.

Current courses in physical education are understandably limited in the time given to biomechanics, but a fuller course in the study of human movement must lay adequate foundations in mathematics and mechanics. Only then is the student well equipped to tackle the many practical and theoretical aspects of the subject, and to cultivate the art of critical appraisal which is so necessary in evaluating developments in a new discipline.

References

1 Cerquiglini, S., 'Evaluation of Athletic Fitness in Weight Lifters through Biomechanical, Bioelectrical and Bioacoustical Data', Rome Seminar, 1971.

2 Chaffin, D. B., 'A Computerised Biomechanical Model—Development

of and Use in Studying Gross Body Action', *J. Biochem. 2*, 1969, 429–41.
3 Daish, C. B., *The Physics of Ball Games*, English Universities Press, 1972.
4 Dyson, G. H. G., *The Mechanics of Athletics*, University of London Press, 1970.
5 French, A. P., *Newtonian Mechanics*, William Clowes, 1971.
6 Grieve, D. W., 'Gait Patterns and the Speed of Walking', *Biomed. Eng. 3,* 1968, 3.
7 Hay, J. G., *The Biomechanics of Sports Techniques*, Prentice-Hall, 1973.
8 Hopper, B. J., *Biomechanics of Human Motion*, Crosby, Lockwood, Staples, 1973.
9 Kane, T. R. and Scher, M. P., 'Human Self-rotation by means of Limb Movements', *J. Biomech. 3*, 1970, 1, 39–49.
10 Kasvand, T., Milner, M. and Rapley, L. F., 'A Computer-based System for the Analysis of some Aspects of Human Locomotion', IMechE Conference on 'Human Locomotor Engineering', University of Sussex, 1971.
11 Kistler Instrument Ltd, *Force Plates and Associated Electronic Equipment*.
12 Miller, D. I. and Nelson, R. C. *Biomechanics of Sport*, Lea & Febiger, 1973.
13 Mitchelson, D. L., 'An Opto-electronic Technique for Analysis of Angular Movements', Rome Seminar, 1971.
14 Plagenhoef, S., *Patterns of Human Motion*, Prentice-Hall, 1971.
15 Ramey, M. R., 'Ise of Force Plates in Long Jump Studies', Rome Seminar, 1971.
16 Smith, A. J., 'A Study of Forces on the Body in Athletic Activities with Particular Reference to Jumping', PhD thesis, University of Leeds, 1972.
17 Tricker, R. A. R. and Tricker, B. J. K., *The Science of Movement*, Elsevier, 1967.

Reference to the Rome Seminar above, and to the seminars at Zürich, Eindhoven and Pennsylvania earlier in the chapter, may be followed up through the published *Proceedings* (Karger, Basle and New York). Some journals containing biomechanical papers are listed below:

Ergonomics
Journal of Applied Physiology
Journal of Biomechanics
Human Factors
Annals of New York Academy of Sciences
Biomedical Engineering
American Journal of Physiology
Research Quarterly
Proceedings of the Royal Society, Series B
Journal of Bone and Joint Surgery
Journal of Human Movement Studies

Astronautics research papers, particularly those from the Wright Patterson Air Force Base, Ohio, bear reference letters AMRL-TR and AMRL-TDR, and may be obtained on microfilm or microfiche from the National Lending Library, Boston Spa, Yorks.

9

Physical education, movement and health

J. G. P. Williams

In the past few decades traditional concepts of physical education have undergone very significant change, and the accent has come to lie more with education through the physical than with education of the physical. However strong may be the educational arguments for this change of accent the consequences have proved in many ways unfortunate, particularly since there is no reason why both concepts should not be equally well served by the same programme and approach.

Physical education in the past has followed the basically simple idea of seeking to produce healthy young bodies as suitable containers for the healthy young minds that were being developed in the classroom. The fact that such an approach gave rise to stereotyped programmes involving some degree of regimentation (and indeed to many forms of physical activity of a more or less compulsory nature which were distasteful to participants) must not be permitted to obscure the fact that despite the manner in which they were sought, the objectives themselves remained valid. Reaction against outmoded methods has tended to be too radical and has resulted in a turn away from the very sound and desirable underlying objectives.

Modern concepts of physical education and human movement, involving as they do accentuation of freedom of movement and expressive patterns of activity have, in keeping with some other forms of educational theory, gone too far in relinquishing the element of control which is essential in all forms of education. It is discipline that acts to convert potential to capacity whether in physical or in mental performance. It is the discipline-induced capability to use body and mind properly and effectively that provides the vehicle for individual expression and fulfilment.

More and more are clinicians coming to realise that the wide range of disabilities known collectively as 'the degenerative locomotor diseases of civilisation' can be attributed to a real lack of body discipline. In the past, many notions of posture and the significance thereof to health have been bandied about. There have been schools of posture as intolerant and bigoted as religious and political ideologies! This has tended to bring into disrepute theories of posture and the importance of posture to health, particularly to the proper use of the body and its protection against degenerative locomotor disease. One consequence has been the withdrawal of many physical educationalists from the task of developing upright and balanced carriage in the young for fear perhaps of becoming labelled with the old disrepute attached to the old postural schools.

In medical terms, the effect seems to have been not only to cause a turn away from postural education but what is worse a turn away from *all* forms of 'remedial' physical education. Teachers of free human movement and physical education in schools tend to concentrate more on athletic skills and expressive activities to the exclusion of dealing effectively with the minor labile orthopaedic complaints which are so amenable to correction within the school physical education programme. The net result is that too many children either receive no corrective physical education at all or (and this is almost as bad) are dragged away from the schoolroom to visit hard-pressed hospital physiotherapy departments intermittently for exercises which cannot thus be effectively supervised over long periods. In consequence our children are becoming less generally fit and demonstrate more orthopaedic abnormalities than is justifiable in the type of civilised society in which we live. It is indeed an indictment of the present state of physical education in schools that when the intake of students to a well-known physical education college was examined medically at the beginning of the year, 30 per cent showed significant clinical abnormalities, the majority of an orthopaedic type which were or could have been amenable to corrective physical exercises. It is because some of the most important developments in recent medical thinking relate to the performance of the human locomotor system that the prevailing attitude of teachers of human movement is so significant, and why signs of a swing back to a more remedial approach are so welcome.

In the past, medical science has had to concentrate very greatly on true disease processes as, indeed, to a considerable extent it still does. For example, cancer, neurological disease and some forms of heart disease still require an immense amount of research and attention. However, many other diseases previously the scourge of the community have come under control—tuberculosis and poliomyelitis are two examples. As a result, clinical science has been free to concentrate more and more attention on the so-called diseases of civilisation and in particular, the degenerative diseases. The role of poor body habit in their cause and of exercise in their prevention and treatment has now become established. Empirical approaches to many of these conditions are no longer relevant. Backache for example is no longer generally and arbitrarily labelled 'prolapsed intervertebral disc' but receives a more accurate analysis of the type of mechanical derangement of the spine involved. A diagnosis such as prolapsed disc is now reserved for those conditions in which the clinical features of the case point unequivocally to one specific clinical state. As soon as thinking of this type takes place, mechanical causes for the derangement are sought. Progressively more attention is being paid in orthopaedics and rehabilitation to the biomechanical side of human locomotor function, and the present rethinking of spinal mechanics in clinical terms has led to a very substantial reappraisal of the methods of treatment available for mechanical derangement of the spine.[1] More important in the present context, however, is the clear understanding engendered of the role of poor body mechanics in the cause of these conditions.

Furthermore, it is becoming progressively clearer that the poor body mechanics responsible are developed at a relatively early age, so that it can with some justice be said that the backache of tomorrow is the fault of the physical educationalist of today! It is not enough for a child to be taught the basic skills of running, jumping, throwing and so on; nor is it enough for the child to learn highly refined movement patterns associated with a particular sport or expressive activity. The demand now is for the development at an early age of biomechanically sound methods of body handling which will protect the child against mechanical derangements of his spine or other parts of his locomotor system in use later in life. In this connection it is interesting to note the extent to which poor body mechanics contributes to injury and breakdown in high-quality athletes and sportsmen committing their bodies to very high workloads. Study of the aetiology of true over-use injuries in sport, especially those areas of sport where highly developed skills are not a factor, indicates very clearly the extent to which these breakdowns are due to poor basic body mechanics.[2]

Peripherally too the relationship between faulty body mechanics and certain clinical syndromes is becoming clearer. Chondromalacia patellae (softening on the underside of the kneecap associated with pain) is a common condition in the young with maximum incidence in the age group 20–30. This condition is a precursor of osteoarthritis. It represents between a quarter and a third of all causes of knee pain in young people, and in its more florid forms can give rise to considerable disability. In the past, it has tended to be treated by various surgical procedures, none of which has proved entirely satisfactory. Recently the very important role of failure of the normal function of the quadriceps mechanism, specifically vastus medialis, has become appreciated although its primary role as a cause of the condition is still in dispute.[3]

None the less, an understanding of the biomechanics of the knee and its supporting musculature has provided a form of treatment which is almost invariably effective if initiated soon enough. Vastus medialis re-education is now recognised as being perhaps the most important single factor in the management of chondromalacia.[4]

In recent years, attention has been focused on joints which tend to give way, usually the ankle or knee joints. For a long time it was recognised that such giving way or instability was associated with actual damage of the supporting ligaments and impaired function in the supporting muscles. Cases have however been observed from time to time, and have become more commonly recognised, in which functional instability can be demonstrated in the presence of intact ligaments—a condition of stable instability.[5] Studies in the ankle and the knee have indicated the importance of the integrity of the proprioceptive feedback mechanism from the joint. Where joint function is significantly impaired in the absence of overt organic damage to the ligaments, muscle re-education and restoration of a satisfactory feedback pattern has become the accepted method of treatment. Previously, stable instability remained unrecognised and therefore inadequately treated, so that affected joints progressed to frank degenerative joint disease. This can now be prevented by appropriate re-education.

Not only is a body awareness and control important in the prevention of disease and injury of the locomotor system but it also has a key role to play in conditions which are quite incidental to normal body habit. Treatment following road traffic, industrial or similar accident is not merely a matter of helping the damaged tissues to heal, it involves also the very important process of reconditioning. With regard to the latter, it has been noted time and time again that the patient's functional recovery is related to his motor educability. The individual with a good concept of his body image and the ability to train and function effectively will rehabilitate far more rapidly than the individual who has no control over his body, no idea of the way in which to move and no concept of a training process. Thus the development of good patterns of movement and good concepts of body activity in the young not only exerts a protective influence in respect of degenerative diseases but also potentially plays a key role in facilitating rehabilitation following accident or injury.

It is not only in respect of the prevention of locomotor injury and disease that good basic training in physical education and human movement is essential. For many years now the role of exercise in the prevention and treatment of disease of the cardiovascular system has been well known. Recent studies have indicated that the liability to such conditions as coronary thrombosis can be reduced in the individual with a fit heart, who takes good exercise regularly, who is able to push his pulse rate up over 150 beats per minute for periods of half an hour daily and whose vital capacity is maintained at over 3 litres.[6] The maintenance of such figures for performance parameters demands a regular pattern of physical exercise, and such exercise is most likely to be carried out or at least carried out effectively by the individual who has found physical activity a pleasant and stimulating experience from the earliest days. Thus the physical educationalist has a further important role to play in conditioning the young to enjoy continued exercise throughout later life.

Looking to the developments to be anticipated over the next few years in relation to the application of discoveries in medicine and allied sciences to human movement studies, the most exciting possibility seems to be that of producing training effects at the ultra-structural level. Recent studies of muscle metabolism and function of the differing components of the muscle cell suggest that it may be possible to plan training programmes for specific tissues in relation to the required activity. Such a concept remains presently in its infancy but the possibilities are considerable.

Perhaps even more important is the scope for development of new understandings and concepts of the psychological basis of performance. For many years it has been apparent that the limits of our present knowledge in respect of physical performance and the training processes that lead towards it are finite. Most people, however, are aware of the enormous potential for psychological engineering in this field. Morehouse in the past has referred to training as a process of 'sensory disinhibition'.[7] The scope for the development of psychological means of motivation is enormous and this area represents an almost uncharted field, the significance of which is apparent, not only in terms of the pure sports performance but of all types of physical activity.

Above all, however, the most important future development will be the closer relationship of the different disciplines of human performance in multi-disciplinary studies and approaches to problems of human activity. Joint studies involving physiologists and clinicians have been the feature of the medical scene for some years, and more recently engineers and bio-engineers have become involved. The next development clearly must be the involvement of teachers of human movement in this multi-disciplinary approach, both at the level of the university where primary research is carried out and at grass-roots level. One seeks again the close liaison of the school medical officer, orthopaedic surgeon and physical educationalist in the better organising of physical education programmes for individual young people and the early recognition and treatment of minor musculo-skeletal defects.[8]

References

1 Newman, P. H. (1968), 'The Spine, the Wood and the Trees', *Proceedings of the Royal Society of Medicine*, *61*, 35.
2 Williams, J. G. P. and Sperryn, P. N. (1972), 'Overuse Injury in Sport and Work', *British Journal of Sports Medicine, 6*, 50.
3 Williams, J. G. P. (1971), 'Diagnostic Pitfalls in the Sportsman's Knee', *Proceedings of the Royal Society of Medicine, 64,* 640.
4 Williams, J. G. P. and Sperryn, P. N. (1976), *Sports Medicine*, 2nd edn, London, Edward Arnold.
5 Freeman, M. A. R. (1965), 'Instability of the Foot after Injuries to the Lateral Ligament of the Ankle', *Journal of Bone and Joint Surgery, 47*B, 669.
6 Fox, S. M., Naughton, J. P. and Corman, P. A. (1972), 'Physical Activity and Cardiovascular Health', *Modern Concepts of Cardiovascular Disease, 46*, 25.

7 Morehouse, L. E. and Rasch, P. J. (1958), *Scientific Basis of Athletic Training*, London, W. B. Saunders Co.
8 Williams, J. G. P. (1965), 'Physical Fitness in Children', in *Physical Medicine in Paediatrics*, ed. Kiernander, London, Butterworths.

10

New directions in psychology of physical education and sport[1]

J. E. Kane

A few years ago Professor F. Musgrove, writing (1968) about curricular objectives, pointed to the fact that certain subjects had entered the curriculum unpretentiously with clear-cut purposes, but then proceeded to elaborate their substantive content and their educational objectives, so that their present claims have become broader, more comprehensive and much more equivocal. Professor Musgrove puts physical education into this category, comparing the relatively simple curricular objectives of 'drill' with the relatively all-embracing claims of its *enfant terrible* which are listed (for example) in the recent Schools Council Enquiry (Kane, 1974) as social awareness, emotional stability, self realisation, aesthetic appreciation, cognitive development, moral development—as well as the rather more expected one of organic development, leisure time activities and motor skills.

Musgrove is right, of course, and we do make it very difficult for those who are attempting to find out what we are trying to do. Indeed this present series of lectures must seem strange to those who have not been following the development and trends over the past few years of physical education and its monarchical academic overlord—'Movement Studies'. Earlier in the series the philosophy, the sociology and the art form of human movement have been considered, both from the academic and professional viewpoints: later on we are to have sessions dealing with the biomechanical analysis of movement, curriculum development in physical education and the assessment of sport in society. In this lecture we are pretentious and bold enough to look at psychological interpretations. What are we up to? And yet to many of us working in colleges and universities for any length of time the field of psychology has been the most attractive and rewarding of disciplines to us in our attempts to understand pure and applied aspects of our work. A short time ago I was pleasantly surprised to have an indirect acknowledgment of the increasing recognition of the psychological interpretations and significance of physical education and sport by way of an invitation from the editor of the *Encyclopaedic Handbook of Medical Psychology* to contribute an article for inclusion in the next edition. Although the editor indicated that my article should find its place in the encyclopaedia under 'S' for Sport, my submission took a rather broad view of sport, so that I was able to touch on psychological aspects that may have more comprehensive relevance in movement studies. This, of course, was the intention of those who set up the International Society of Sport Psychology in Rome in 1964. On that occasion a number of psychologists, physical educators and others met to discuss psychological perspectives of man's physical activities exemplified in his games, play, dance and sporting involvement.

The *Proceedings* of this conference (Antonelli, 1966) were published as a 1,300-page monograph and represent an important statement of the various dimensions of sports psychology. The Second International Congress of Sport Psychology was held in Washington in 1968, and led to the publication of another impressive proceedings under the title *Contemporary Psychology of Sport* (Kenyon, 1970). National societies for those interested in sports psychology have been founded in recent years in more than thirty countries, and it is reported (Vanek and Cratty, 1970) that a number of European universities have chairs in the discipline of sports psychology.

Sports psychology, then, may be regarded as an area of study which is concerned with the application of psychological knowledge to learning, performance and associated behaviour in the context of man's physical activities—his games, play, dance and sporting involvements. It has its foundations, therefore, in many areas of psychology and psychiatry from where it seeks meaning, interpretation and understanding. The main areas of psychology which appear to be most interesting and rewarding to the sports psychologist might seem to be, for example, learning, motivation, perception, personality, mental health and social psychology. However, for the purposes of this paper I shall have to be very selective.

I have decided to consider, for the rest of the time available to me, the present trends and, as I see them, some future possibilities in the application of certain areas of psychological knowledge to physical education and sport. In this undertaking I have had to choose to include certain considerations and exclude others. In the event I decided to exclude any serious account of the psychomotor learning process, which to many may seem surprising. I have done this for two reasons. In the first place I consider that most of you are probably better acquainted with the experimental and theoretical literature relating to skills learning and teaching than to almost any other area of psychology, and you will therefore be aware of the relatively huge volume of recent published works, especially those speculating on the structure of the human information processing system, which is awaiting a synthesis and specific application to the acquisition and teaching of gross skills. The most formidable but potentially the most rewarding immediate task here may be to interpret Broadbent's (1971) *Decision and Stress*. My second reason for giving little more than a passing reference to the mechanistic aspects of motor learning is that I feel there are other equally attractive possibilities for emphasis which have, to my way of thinking, a great deal of importance in behavioural interpretations of our work, but which have had less serious consideration in our literature.

I intend, therefore, to make only a few brief references to work on the perceptual-motor process, and then to proceed to comment on a few studies concerning abilities and learning, personality, motivation and body experience.

Perceptual-motor process

The main stream of thinking on skilled performance considers the individual as an information processing system in which the essential and linked elements are

(a) a perceptual system through which information is filtered and coded
(b) a translatory mechanism which has limited decision-making capacity, and
(c) an effector mechanism controlling response.

Various feedback loops are proposed to relate these elements and the memory stores. Welford's (1968) hypothetical block diagram of the human sensory-motor system is shown (Figure 10.1) as an attractive explanation based on various researches in perception, choices, movement and memory. More recently Broadbent (1971) has added a great deal of additional detailed information and speculation, while Whiting (1970) has contributed a most helpful interpretation of the linked processes involved in the learning and performance of ball skills. The recent writings in this area are fascinating for the physical educationist and will assuredly repay careful attention. Two brief examples taken from Broadbent's work may be indicative of explanations that will prove useful in understanding skilled performance.

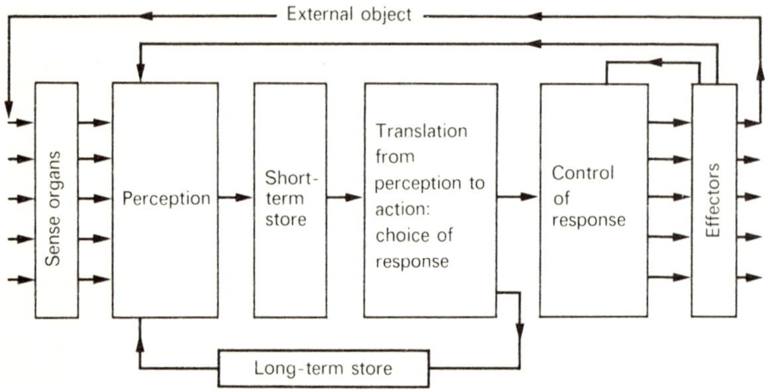

Figure 10.1 Hypothetical diagram of the human sensory-motor system showing some of the feedback loops (Welford, 1968)

1 Selective process

It has been argued for some time now that because of the limitations of the sense organs and the amount of information present in any display, it becomes necessary for attention and perception to be selective. The ability to select out relevant stimuli and ignore irrelevant ones is apparently learned and presumably susceptible to teaching and coaching. Broadbent has recently suggested a second major selective process called 'pigeonholing' which is proposed to describe the method by which the output (or category states) from the channel is also subjected to selective control, comparable with the 'filtering' procedure at the input of the channel. He does in fact also propose a third selective process—'categorising'—which affects both input and output and is described as a relatively slow, long-term process which appears to deal with 'conditional probabilities of past events'. These elaborations regarding the selective processes appear to make a great deal of sense for the understanding of motor skills learning, since they take account of recall from earlier experience transferability and other factors affecting selectivity of action.

It would appear that any further knowledge of gross skills acquisition will depend greatly on an organised approach to the way in which these selective processes may work in the particular situations that arise in physical education and sport.

2 Channel capacity

It is reassuring to know from Broadbent (1971) that it is now possible to do two things at once! In 1958 Broadbent observed that, in accordance with the notion of a limited single channel for the transmission of information 'a view of attention as unitary might also be taken to mean that man cannot perform two tasks at once: which experimental evidence shows to be untrue'. His current statement on this point is that 'tasks with low information content can be carried out simultaneously without too much impairment'. He illustrates this point by asking the reader to consider the position of a car driver on a familiar route who can easily carry on a casual conversation (when the geographical and conversation probabilities of what is to follow are high and the information correspondingly low) with the position of the same driver in unfamiliar traffic conditions and attempting to follow an abstruse argument (where the probabilities are low and the information high). In the second case the performance in one or both tasks must suffer—but as Broadbent adds 'the limitation is on information not on stimulation'. The implication of these newer notions of the system's ability to process information would seem to be apposite for the teacher and coach, especially with respect to the load limit of information in learning skills and to the way the load is related to previous experience, motor educability, kinaesthetic sensitivity and maturation.

Abilities and learning

1 Integrated development

Ismail (1968) and his colleagues have, in recent years, assiduously researched the link between motor aptitude and abilities in other domains, for example, academic achievement, emotional development and social development. In each case significant associations across domains have been established so that Ismail has proposed a theory of integrated development which is based on stronger experimental grounds than earlier versions of developmental theories emphasising the interaction of hereditary maturational and environmental influences. In the process, Ismail's researches have demonstrated the way in which motor aptitudes (especially those emphasising co-ordination) and intellectual aptitudes are linked, and he provides somewhat frighteningly long regression equations to predict academic scores from certain motor aptitude scores. What is even more intriguing is that the factor structures explaining the interaction between these two domains hold good cross-culturally. He and I found almost identical factor structures for London children as he had done for US children. Clearly a lot more study is required to clarify the way in which children's movement ability may be linked with other abilities and capacities. Not only that but, as Kephart remarks in his introduction to Ismail's book, 'if these studies by Ismail are found on replication and elaboration to produce consistent results then a new dimension in the learning process will open up for the motor aptitude domain'. The emphasis on the learning process by Kephart is interesting since a number of researchers and teachers have recently attested to the particular value of the motor performance route for contributing significantly to learning and achievement in other areas (see, e.g. Cratty (1972), Oliver (1960), Kephart (1960) and Humphrey (1973)).

2 Earlier and later learning

The usual finding has been that early in motor learning various perceptual factors make a more significant contribution to learning and performance than do motor factors. At the final stages, however, it is the motor or movement factor that appears to assume paramount importance. In perhaps the most important study yet reported on this issue, Fleishman (1964) identified the amount of variance accounted for at different stages in the practice of a discrimination RT task by such variables as RT, rate of movement, psychomotor co-ordination, dexterity, perceptual accuracy, mechanical experience, spatial relations, discrimination reaction time specific. He found, as predicted, that as the task was mastered movement capacities (e.g. movement speed, movement rate and RT) exerted more influence upon performance. He also found—and this I think is very important—that the application of these findings could significantly affect terminal learning by the insertion at appropriate points of instruction cues. It seems highly likely that the learning of many motor skills could benefit from this kind of analysis and subsequent instructional guide.

3 Developmental issues

It seems surprising to me that so little has been written in the movement studies literature concerning the way in which the work of Piaget and Bruner (for example) in the field of development psychology might be related to the learning and acquisition of motor abilities. There appears to be a wealth of theories and speculation from this area of psychology that on the face of it appears to have enlightening possibilities for those committed to movement education. I am happy to say, however, that I am aware of four research studies in the movement area attempting to test hypotheses emanating from the writings of Piaget and Bruner. I am even happier to say that two of them are currently being undertaken at the West London Institute of Higher Education. I shall discuss one of them. The starting point is the hunch that a 'movement' approach to learning may facilitate cognitive growth and development in certain ways, by operating another learning channel and giving to the child an additional vehicle for knowing and understanding. The specific springboard for the study is Bruner's point that there is a need for preparation of experience and mental operations before language can be used effectively in problem-solving operations, and he goes on to suggest that 'language' and 'experience' operate independently of each other until a child has attained the rules and 'surplus meaning' of language. Language and understanding are not therefore always congruent, and what is said will often represent a 'mis-match' with what is seen and understood. The hypothesis is then that by broadening and elaborating the experience of the pre-operational child through appropriate movement opportunities, he will develop an additional and meaningful movement language which will help him to understand better the meaning of such semantic terms as (for example), more, less, larger, smaller, etc., which in turn will improve his problem-solving ability. In particular the study is assessing the effect of developing the child's movement awareness in (for example), feeling or becoming larger, wider, etc. on the development of concepts of conservation. The findings are anticipated with interest.

4 Reminiscence

In laboratory tasks of a repetitive nature Eysenck has consistently found improvements in performance (and presumably in learning) after a rest period. This phenomenon called reminiscence has been explained as both a consolidation of the memory trace during rest (i.e. learning) and as the reduction in reactive inhibition which gives rise to better performance. It is debatable whether the findings with respect to reminiscence found in the limited laboratory situations for repetitive tasks which may lead to boredom and mental fatigue may be translated into the gross motor-skill learning situations in which physical fatigue is often a factor, but certainly the possibilities of showing unexpected improvements in learning by the judicious manipulation of work and rest period seem too good to miss for the want of trying out.

Personality and sport

It is an assumption long held by physical educationists and coaches that there exists a link between an individual's personality and his athletic or sports aptitude and ability. One argument is that the athletics environment constitutes an ideal setting for the development of desirable personality characteristics such as confidence, sociability, self-reliance and general adjustment. Another line of reasoning has come from coaches who intuitively are apparently aware of the personality variables in predicting performance. Cofer and Johnson (1960) even suggested that in their personality structure athletes represent 'a special breed', and Ogilvie and Tutko (1966) as most of you will already be aware, claim to have identified the personality dimensions which are essential to competitive success.

Recently the interest in research attempting to relate personality to athletics, sports and general motor ability has greatly increased, due no doubt to the improved validity of the measures available. A number of recent broad-based researches (e.g. Fleishman, 1964) have begun to give increasing clarity and dependability to our notion of the factors involved in gross physical ability and, at the same time, procedures for assessing personality have become theoretically sounder, more meaningful and better standardised, even if personality theory still appears to be 'a disconcerting sprawl'.

The increasing use being made of the Cattell 16 PF and the Eysenck EPI has had the advantage of allowing some comparison of findings from different research in this area, though major conceptual and experimental problems remain, and these clearly require urgent attention if generalisations are to be made. In particular criticism has consistently been correctly levelled at sampling procedures, inappropriate methods of data analysis and the general dearth of clearly formulated hypotheses. Nevertheless, a number of useful reviews of the empiric research are available, and from these it would seem that a basis exists for further rigorous research. These reviews give a general personality description of the male athlete in terms of his extrovert tendencies (e.g. dominance, social aggression and tough-mindedness) and emotional control. Women athletes are most often described as being like men athletes on the extroversion dimension, but being unlike them in showing a higher level of emotional lability. There are, of course, many exceptions to these general descriptions based on mean ratings, and no doubt both the nature of the sport in question and the level of participation will in some way affect the individual's characteristic way of behaving. The way in which the control of these two critical variables has helped to clarify the description of athletes into 'personality types' is developed elsewhere (Kane, 1972). In a more general way the usefulness of information about an athlete's position on the two main personality dimensions, namely extroversion/introversion and emotionality has also been repeatedly pointed out. The relationship of these dimensions to variability of performance, pain tolerance, conditioning and lability to stress has been documented by Eysenck (1965) and deserves the closest attention of those concerned with maximising the performance of athletes.

There have been, however, some attempts to take a stage further the study of the personality relationship with athletic ability. A few examples will have to suffice. Kroll (1969) for example took research in this area to a new level when he demonstrated in a number of studies the value of discriminant function analysis for comparing personality profiles of athletes representing winning and losing team, different sport and levels of achievement in the same sport. The hypotheses developed from the descriptive studies that male athletes tend to be stable extroverts and women athletes somewhat more anxious extroverts has recently been strengthened by correlational evidence involving a number of multivariate techniques (Kane, 1972). The studies by Tattersfield (1971) have thrown a new light on the vexed question of possible personality changes as a result of involvement in athletic sports. The few longitudinal studies on adults that have been reported are in accord in finding little or no personality change over time in those who have been followed for three or four years. Tattersfield, however, has demonstrated significant change in 'age-group' swimmers between the ages of 10 and 14 years compared with matched controls. The changes over time were towards greater extroversion, less emotionality (anxiety) and more dependency. From an educational standpoint it may be considered that the first and second of these personality changes would not be interpreted as undesirable, but the third one—toward greater dependency—most certainly would.

Kroll (1969), among others, has considered the possible future approaches and techniques that may prove rewarding in the area of research attempting to clarify the relationship between personality and sports performance. He points in particular to a number of alternative approaches to the formation of testable hypotheses which will repay the careful attention of those wishing to take our understanding beyond the purely descriptive dimensions of the problem.

In addition to Kroll's suggestions there are possibly a number of other approaches that might well be considered. Conceptually the Allport (1963) description of behaviour as an admixture of 'coping' and 'expressive' aspects is attractive to those interested in the broader interpretations of human movement and non-verbal communication. On the face of it there does seem to be a different personality requirement necessary for effective coping with, for example, certain precisely defined skills, and the qualities needed for interpretation and bodily communication in expressive tasks in, for example, dance and some forms of sport.

Although the admitted purpose of personality assessment is to predict behaviour in given situations, the observed behaviour of athletes in the intense competitive situation is often found to be at variance with his observed behaviour and measured personality outside the sporting context. This has led some researchers to look carefully at what they call 'situationally-specific' behaviour. The difficulties involved here are technically and experimentally great, but this has not daunted the efforts of a number of researchers at Penn State University, and their interesting initial probes must surely encourage others to join in this valuable work. One of the notions coming from these Penn State University studies is that there is a difference (among women at least) between the 'sporting self' and the 'social self'. One of the most important factors affecting sports performance is the player's ability to handle stress, and his behaviour in stressful situations is no doubt a product of his standing on source (or 'resting') anxiety, and his lability to anxiety arousal to a given stress. Speilberger's (1966) postulation of 'trait' and 'state' anxiety seems to be a particularly suitable basis for interpretation and hypothesis building with respect to the athletes' behaviour in and out of the competitive sports situation.

The problem of understanding behaviour in the sports situation may be reduced by an approach to personality which emphasises its dynamic nature in the interaction between the persona and the environment which is largely ignored in broad trait typologies. For this reason attention to the dispositions which lead to typical responses rather than the responses themselves may be vitally important in this area of research. The dispositional approach to personality acknowledges the influence of the individual's psychological field on his reaction to stimuli. It is, therefore, concerned with the individual's 'cognitive style' in his interpretation of situations and his interaction with them. Among dispositions which have been studied as aspects of personality are authoritarianism, dogmatism, manifest anxiety, achievement motivation, machiavellianism, social desirability, persuasability. Each of these embodies a conception of personality which involves both cognitive and behavioural dimensions.

Cognitive style or the individual's stereotypic way of perceiving and the related links with psychological functioning has for a long time been researched by Witkin (1962) and his colleagues. Those interested in learning and performance in perceptual motor risks of the sort commonly experienced in sport have recently found increasing insight from Witkin's interpretations. The attraction is that Witkin's notions are based on body image and body concept, from which he argued a connection between the individual's generalised way of experiencing body, self and the surrounding world. The thesis is developed to distinguish between those who typically experience the body as distinct from the surrounding field (i.e. 'field-dependent'). Attention has been drawn (Kane, 1972) to the possible links between Poulton's classification of skills into 'open skills' (in which the reading of the environmental display is vital) and 'closed skills' (in which there is relative independence of environmental stimuli) and Witkin's perceptual styles based on field dependence–independence.

Highly consistent sex differences in field dependence–independence have been found (Witkin, 1962). In particular women make large errors compared with men in their perception of bodily positions and in identifying a hidden figure within a complex design, being misled relatively easily by the surrounding visual field. Consequently they tend to be described more often as field-dependent.

Jones (1970) in a most interesting personality study of English women physical education majors found them, as a group, to be field-independent, and significantly more so than the norms for American women. This is not altogether unexpected. The study involved the use of a number of personality assessments which, when subjected to factor analysis, revealed that the major portion of the personality variance accounted for among these women students was made up of 15 per cent extroversion, 13 per cent emotionality (anxiety), 9 per cent superego strength, 7 per cent field dependence–independence, and 7 per cent toughmindedness. Jones's findings, using the Eysenck PI concerning the general personality description of these physical education majors, was in accord with Kane's (1972) conclusion that women in sport were relatively extroverted and anxious.

Motivation and performance

It is an attractive exercise for those of us interested in human movement (particularly as exemplified in sports, play and dance) to go through the various well-established theories of motivation, and consider how each might be applied to our problems. I have played this game myself and have reported my views, but in all honesty I cannot say that the effort was worth it (Kane 1968). Nevertheless, I share to some extent the enthusiasm of many for Maslow's hierarchy of motives ranging from the lower level of physiological needs through drives of security, safety and belonging to those based on a need for respect, on top of which is placed the capping monarchical need for 'self-actualisation'. At the highest level Maslow's hierarchy identifies the need for the realisation of the individual's capacities and potentialities, presumably through the pursuit of excellence. Such a concept is appealing to those who try to explain the drive to excellence in sport. We would, however, have to explain the sustaining satisfaction of the average person for continued involvement in some other way—perhaps as either an example of Allport's 'functional autonomy' or more basically a Hullian 'activity drive'.

Some of the more recent attempts to account for motivation have appeared to have more applicability to involvement and performance in sport. Helson (1959) related motivation specifically to performance in his hypothesis of par or tolerance. The hypothesis is that in most tasks individuals set their standards or aspirations habitually below the level of performance they could achieve. Left to his own devices man will apparently often stop short of his capability. If this is so the implications for sport might be that appropriate and relevant standards need to be set by the teacher or coach. Moreover, it would seem that without such motivation one can only speculate on the validity of, say, fitness testing and the associated norms that are published as a guide to standards. Of course, the effect of previous successes and failure will determine to some extent the level of acceptable performance in related contexts. Littig (1967) found that males were relatively unaffected across conditions of reward, punishment or neutrality, whereas females learned trigrams quicker under either reward or punishment. The reward conditions were positive and helpful reactions from the experimenter, and punishment was applied through negative statements such as 'You're a slow learner' and 'My God, you students are dumb'. The females were reported as learning more rapidly than males under these negative 'punishment' conditions. In general, however, it seems that females tend to set easier goals for themselves than males and persevere less under task difficulty and stress. Wyrick (1971) reports a study of males and females on both a simple and a difficult task. All the subjects were permitted to succeed on the simple task, but were stopped before they had time to finish the difficult task. On the following day the subjects were given the choice of continuing the difficult task until they solved it, or repeating the simple task. The males chose the difficult task, and the females the simple one.

Dember and Earl (1957) suggested a 'new look' model in motivation which Earl (1961) later expressed in rigorous detail. They emphasised the nature of goal objects and in particular focused attention on their complexity value of stimuli as the critical variable. The individual himself also has a complexity level called his 'ideal' which may change with maturation and experience. It is the relationship between the individual's 'ideal' complexity level and that of a stimulus that determines its incentive value for him. Stimuli that lie closest to the 'ideal' will be preferred. A special place and function is given in the model for those stimuli that are, in complexity value, just above the 'ideal'. The hyper-attractive stimuli are called pacers, which function to raise an individual's complexity level in the process of coping with them. As pacers serve to bring the individual up to their level they eventually do themselves out of a job, their function being replaced by pacers of an even higher complexity.

For our purpose in sport the Dember–Earl model of motivation seems to have held all kinds of useful and operational possibilities. Locating the right pacers and pitching them at the right level with respect to previous experience and success would, no doubt, provide the real test.

Achievement motivation is one of the widely studied dispositional approaches to the basic understanding of behaviour. The motive to succeed is claimed to be a major determinant of striving competitive behaviour towards standards of excellence. Those high in need to achieve show a major concern with doing something well and tend to be independent and persistent; hence it might seem that people of this kind will be attracted to competitive athletics. McClelland (1961) and Atkinson (1964) have described in detail the characteristics and sources of the achievement need, and have reported incidentally that in their assessment of proliterate societies they found a clear link between achievement need and the incidence of competitive and individualistic games playing.

A considerable amount of research evidence suggests that achievement motivation is learned at an early stage and becomes a relatively stable aspect of behaviour. Atkinson for instance found that subjects with a high need for achievement (Nach) performed better on tasks requiring individual initiative, but not on routine group tasks. Feather (1967) contends that those with high Nach tend to direct and take responsibilities for outcomes, while those with low Nach tend to regard outcomes as inevitable and beyond their control. In a study by Weiner and Kukla (1970) the subjects were divided into two groups on Nach—those above and those below the median. All subjects were then set the problem of guessing in several instances the next number in a series. The actual outcomes of the problems were determined by chance so that ability was not involved. When the tests were completed the subjects were asked to estimate how many of the points they scored were due to 'skill' rather than 'guessing'. The high Nach group showed a wide variation in points scored, and reported that they attributed their successes to skill and their failures to lack of skill—even though their scores were in fact due to chance. The low Nach group demonstrated less variation and did not attribute the outcome of the tests to personal characteristics.

Bardwick (1971) argues that the achievement motivation model as represented by McClelland and Atkinson does not hold good for women. She quotes Atkinson as giving only a footnote to women and referring to the differences between the sexes as being 'perhaps the most persistent unresolved problem in research on need achievement'. It is true that the initial research was undertaken at a college for males, and that several subsequent attempts to use the Nach measures on female students met with disappointing results. For example, while the Nach results for men helped to predict certain achievement-related performances, the relationship for women was negligible. Dember (1970) suggests that the test procedures for successfully inducing achievement motivation among men may be inappropriate for women, and he also proposes the alternative explanation that women college students are already at such a chronically high level of achievement motivation that little room is left for experimental manipulation. Bardwick (1971) looks at it differently. She maintains that among women the need to achieve is inextricably linked with another need—that of affiliation—so that in their case the motive to achieve may be affected by the expectation of the reaction of significant others with respect to praise, blame, love, acceptance, rejection, etc. Her point of view is summarised in the following excerpt from her book: 'Does a person strive to achieve because he has an internal standard of excellence, a self-image and feeling of self-esteem dependent on how he perceives himself performing—or does he achieve primarily in order to receive praise from others?' In answer to the question we have the suggestion of Verhoff (1969) that for boys the achievement motive is set off by internalised notions related to standards of excellence, while for girls external support is to be regarded as critical.

The achievement-oriented person is apparently attracted by risk, though some research shows that the high achiever takes only moderate risks and avoids excessive ones. According to McClelland and Atkinson, risk-taking is one of the more salient types of behaviour on which achievement motivation is likely to impinge. The theoretical formulation of the relationship between achievement motivation and risk-taking (cf. Atkinson and Feather, 1966) identifies firstly two decision-making components, subjective probability (P) and incentive (I) which are placed in direct inverse relationship to each other. If, for instance, a task is easy the subjective probability of success (Ps) will be high and the incentive value (Is) correspondingly low. A person undertaking such a task would, according to the theory, get little satisfaction from success. On the other hand a person who solves a very difficult problem (where the probability of success was low) presumably is immensely pleased. The counterparts of Ps and Is are Pf and If, which represent the subjective probability and the incentive value of failure, and the model assumes that the probabilities of success and failure add up to one.

The model also includes two kinds of motivation construction—a motive to achieve success (Ms) and a motive to avoid failure (Mf). Both motives are considered to be present in all people though the strength will vary from person to person so that in some $Ms > Mf$, while in others $Mf < Ms$, and in others still $Ms = Mf$. These two motives combine with the decision-making components of probability and incentive in achievement-oriented situations to account for the extent of the risk-taking behaviour. The resultant motivation is expressed in terms of a tendency to approach success or a tendency to avoid failure, and may be expressed in the following form:

$$\text{Resultant motivation} = (Ms \times Ps \times Is = \text{Approach}) + (Mf \times Pf \times If = \text{Avoidance})$$

The 'approach' component is always positive and the 'avoidance' component is always negative since If is always taken to be negative—failure being always regarded as undesirable. It can be seen that if $Ms = Mf$, the resultant would equal zero, and the individual's action would be determined by other motives altogether. If $Ms > Mf$ all resulting actions will be positive, but strongest where $Ps = 0 \cdot 5$, giving rise to the general rule of the model that individuals in whom the motive to succeed is salient will be attracted to tasks of intermediate difficulty. If, however, $Mf < Ms$, there will be a tendency to avoidance in all tasks which will be most negative where $P = 0 \cdot 5$, and least negative for extreme values of P. Such individuals will, therefore, tend to avoid moderate tasks and make either extremely risky decisions or extremely conservative ones.

Willis and Bethe (1970) consider the implications of this kind of model to tasks in physical education and sport and point to a number of conceptual and methodological difficulties which need resolving before the model can be used. On the other hand they do indicate that certain adaptations of the model have proved to be useful as predictors of performance. There seems little doubt that the model could form a very useful basis for assessing motivation and decision-making in the sporting context, but equally it seems clear that a great deal of careful research is needed before it can be regarded as operationally sound.

Arousal and performance

In spite of the difficulties in obtaining valid and stable measures of arousal, a great deal of empiric evidence has been established for a relationship between arousal or activation level and psychological processes, especially performance. The way in which arousal level in a given situation represents a chronic autonomic disposition and/or a susceptibility or lability reaction is not well understood, but it seems certain that motivational forces differentially affect individuals' behaviour. Lacey (1959) proposed in fact two types of people with respect to their patterns of fluctuation in autonomic arousal level—stabiles and labiles. Stabiles showed an even, quiet, unchanging autonomic functioning, while labiles showed greater variability, involving spontaneous bursts of physiological activity. In terms of related behaviour Lacey hypothesised that labiles would be impulsive in motor activity, would for instance find difficulty in withholding incorrect responses, and would tend to be in general more susceptible to external stimuli.

The way in which performance is linked with arousal level or activation has been well documented by Duffy (1962), and the generalised proposition is that the relationship is best expressed by an inverted U-shaped curve in which performance improves with arousal from a low level up to an optimum, after which performance deteriorates with further increases in arousal. From the motivational point of view we are interested not only in the specific way in which arousal level goes with performance, but also in the way in which a given level of arousal is constituted. It has been argued (Kane, 1972) that we might consider two interacting constituent components—chronic arousal factor, reflecting stimulation, and arousability, describing the general lability of the autonomic system. Such an explanation allows the identification of a relatively stable personality factor and a variable reactivity factor, concerned with individual lability to arousal-producing situations and with arousal modulation. Motives and their related drives may be considered in this explanation to affect both factors, since they may shape both the personality and the extrinsic situational circumstances which cause arousal. If indeed motivation has such a pervasive effect on arousal it is not surprising that much of the empiric research in our field has produced equivocal results. Some workers for instance have found that certain motivational procedures produce better physical performances, while others have concluded that all procedures improve performance, but no significant difference between procedures exists, and yet others have suggested that motivational procedures don't seem to improve performance at all (cf. Oxendine, 1968). If, however, we accept the notion that motivation follows an inverted-U relationship with performance, we can expect a low to optimum motive intensity to give rise to better performance, but beyond the optimum level increased motivation will show poorer returns in performance. What we need to know, therefore, is the level of arousal generated by a particular intensity of motivation. Only by knowing this will we be able to suggest whether subsequent motivation should be increased or decreased to produce optimal performance (cf. Kane, 1972).

Application to sport

In the application of theories of motivation to performance in sport much speculation and discussion has centred round the terms intrinsic and extrinsic. No doubt the athlete who strives for perfection is driven by a mixture of intrinsic and extrinsic motives—motives which, on the one hand, derive from the individual's ego needs and personal gratification, and on the other, have their source in the concern the individual has with pleasing others. While not wishing to de-emphasise the primacy of the central core of intrinsic motivation, it is important to recognise the significance and potency of extrinsic motives. More to the point, it seems inevitable that the admixture of intrinsic and extrinsic motives changes, and that an activity or behaviour generated initially by one kind of drive may be continued for another. Consider, for example, the substance of a hypothetical individual who joins the local golf club for essentially social reasons, but who, once he has become reasonably competent at the game, intensifies his golfing activities for intrinsic motives of satisfaction in coping successfully. If he later becomes highly skilled and enters tournaments, it may be that extrinsic motives of financial rewards, social recognition, etc., have become paramount again. Knapp (1963) makes the point in the context of sport skills that since activities which are too easy pall, and that those that are too difficult are abandoned, the optimum performance therefore might itself be conceived as a moving point on a scale from the early stages to the later stages of practice, and 'might be best considered as a percentage improvement to be aimed at'. As progress becomes more difficult the rungs of the 'success' ladder might then be structured closer together. Concerning the motivational effect of the 'too easy' and the 'too difficult', Allport said, 'It seems to be neither the perfected talent nor the automatic habit that has the driving power, but the imperfect talent and the habit-in-the-making . . . the active motive subsides when its goal is reached, or in the case of a motor skill, when it has at last become automatic.'

The strength and efficacy of motive force in effecting skilled performance is, for the reasons outlined above, difficult to quantify. Performance is, in some as yet ill-defined way, the outcome of ability (or skill) and motivation. If, as Gagne and Fleishman (1959) believe, performance is the product of skill and motivation then, provided both elements are present in some quantity, the one can compensate for the other so that presumably a given level of performance may be achieved by, for example, either the combination of high skill and low motivation, or the combination of low skill and high motivation. This seems an unlikely explanation over a wide range of skilled sports ability, but it may have some relevance within narrow limits of skill, and rather more relevance in tasks with a low skill element.

However, in spite of the difficulties inherent in explaining the way in which motivation and skill interact in performance, there is no shortage of writers in physical education and sport who acknowledge the central importance of motivation in accounting for differences in sports performance.

Practically all the hypotheses and speculations in the area of sports motivation have come, not surprisingly, from the study of groups, and even with appropriate caveats, allowing for inter-individual variance, such an approach may miss catching the unique motives and meaning of specific behaviour by a particular individual. The difficulties and dangers of coaches and teachers making behavioural interpretations and predictions for one athlete, on the basis of a single personality or motivational profile derived from one of the standard questionnaires, have often been emphasised, even though Cattell (1965) makes certain claims for the value of comparing an individual's profile with a criterion profile and utilising the resulting coefficient of similarity as an index for occupational selection. At the other extreme, as it were, Beisser (1967) emphasises the value of a clinical psychoanalytic approach based on the expert's interpretation of an individual athlete's behavioural problems. It is not my wish to enter the debate on the theoretical soundness, nor the operational effectiveness of clinical psychology and psychiatry, but just to indicate that there is an approach to the explanation of motivated behaviour which considers the individual as a unique functioning system. In a real sense, therefore, we are confronted with the dilemma surrounding the nomothetic versus the ideographic controversy. Nomothetic approaches tend to look for general laws in behaviour that are generally applicable, whereas the ideographic takes the line that each individual is a law unto himself. It does not seem to be unreasonable to expect, in the search for motivational explanations for athletic performance, that both nomothetic and ideographic approaches will have a contribution to make. Ogilvie and Tutko have jointly contributed such a two-pronged approach to the problem.

In their earlier work Ogilvie and Tutko (1966) emphasised intrinsic motives in athletic behaviour, especially ego satisfaction arising from an athlete's internalised sense of pride in his own ability, and they considered that each athlete represented in behaviour a unique admixture of motives. These researchers then applied their clinical experience to the problem and proceeded to describe and explain certain clinical syndromes of problem athletes' behaviour in such terms as 'success phobic', 'depression-prone' and 'toughminded immature'. The insights developed as a result of these approaches enabled Ogilvie and Tutko to suggest forms of 'therapy' which coaches might use with 'non-realisers of potential'. Subsequently work has led through a wider nomothetic investigation of the elite athletics population to the development of the Athletic Motivation Inventory, which is structured in two categories measuring respectively the strength of athletes' intentions or desires, and their emotionality. Intention or desire is assessed by questions aimed at measuring drive, aggression, determination, leadership and organisation. Emotionality, regarded as the major factor in assessing an athlete's reaction to stress, is rated by responses to questions related to his coachability, self-confidence, emotional maturity, conscience development, trust and mental toughness. The authors of the AMI abrogate to themselves at present the sole responsibility for the interpretation and meaning of scores (presumably on the basis of norms) on their instrument. No doubt when a manual of the AMI is published a full assessment will be made of the theoretical foundations, validity and operational usefulness of this especially structured approach to the understanding of athletic motivation. In the meantime we can acknowledge Ogilvie and Tutko's efforts to get the best from both 'worlds'—the nomothetic and the ideographic. Concerning the position of women athletes with respect to the AMI, I imagine we can assume that the sub-factor scales listed above hold good equally for women. This assumption seems reasonable, following the inclusion of the AMI in the study by Williams *et al.* (1970) of women fencers, but it would be fascinating to study (and compare with men) the norms for women athletes on all the twelve explanatory factors, but particularly on the five factors purporting to explain the direction and strength of the drive to compete at a high level.

Almost no rigorous empiric evidence exists by which we may accurately assess the type of motives that explain adult involvement in—or lack of involvement in—athletic sports and other physical activities. No one set of explanatory theories is likely to be satisfactory, since it seems reasonable to expect that for those who are involved, at whatever level, there are differential inducements. The hope is that here, as in so many other areas of our work, we may see an increase in the volume of fundamental research. One encouraging and exciting experimental lead is currently being given by Dr Pearl Berlin (1972). Her recent report gives details of hypothesised motives for women's involvement in sport with a distinction being drawn between what are termed 'individual' and 'situational' motive effects. On the basis of initial Q-sort reactions from women students the investigators feel able to identify three areas of situational effects—those contributing to self-regard and opportunities to develop both mastery and dynamic interaction—and five individual incentive areas related to stress-seeking, accomplishing, gratifying, affiliating and gaining recognition. The further development and clarification of this model is eagerly anticipated.

Body concept

The body and its reactions are fundamental concerns in physical education. The vocabulary is full of terms which reflect the central concern with the body—body development, body sensitivity, body awareness, body control, body expression. It would seem, therefore, that an appreciation of body psychology, especially body image—and its implications for self-image and self-concept—may be of particular importance to the physical educator who anticipates the psychological outcomes from his work which the literature suggests. Indeed, there does appear to be a substantial amount of indirect support to suggest that movement experiences may lead to a more sensitive, articulated and satisfying development of the body which in turn may critically shape personality. Freud emphasised the point in commenting that 'the ego is first and foremost a bodily ego'. It seems that concepts of self and body are very closely linked, due no doubt to the unique closeness of the individual's body to himself as a perceiver. His body is the only object in his perceptual field which is at once perceived by him, and is also part of himself.

Elsewhere I have listed and discussed the importance to physical educationists of a number of the interrelated elements that may go to form body concept (Kane, 1972). Among those regularly referred to in the psychological literature and which, on the face of it, seem to have immediate relevance are body orientation in space, body boundary, body cathexis and body type. The first of these, body orientation in space, is part of the Witkin hypothesis mentioned earlier by which it is proposed that psychological differentiation in general and an individual's idiosyncratic way of perceiving in particular is related to his personality. One of Witkin's major propositions is that the extent to which the body concept is more or less articulated is associated with a tendency to experience the self and the surroundings in a similar way, and is reflected in a 'style of life'.

The body boundary concept proposed by Fisher and Cleveland (1958) suggests that body image depends on the individual's perception of his body boundaries. Individuals apparently vary in the extent to which they experience their bodies as being clearly and sharply bounded and secure from what is 'out there'. The strength of this boundary may be assessed as a 'barrier score' or as a 'penetrability score'.

Jourard and Secord (1954) focused attention on the individual's satisfaction (or cathexis) towards the body and its parts. These authors found significant links between body cathexis and self cathexis, ranging from 0·58 for males to 0·66 for females. They also undertook most interesting studies of body satisfaction and dissatisfaction among men and women and reported in the *Journal of Abnormal Psychology* on 'Body Cathexis and the Ideal Female Figure'.

Body type is too well understood a concept for me to elaborate on it here. However, recent studies do add something of a new dimension. It appears that there is a well-embedded stereotyped social perception of physiques (favouring the mesomorph) in relation to behaviour and acceptability. Such a stereotype must undoubtedly affect the way in which an individual perceives his physique and himself.

The importance of these four elements of body image and body concept is apparent. They may represent interrelated aspects of ego foundation. In this connection the implications for physical education may be critical in that it is centrally concerned with the body, and with 'body awareness' in the broadest psychological meaning of that term. It may well be that 'body awareness' as used in physical education must be considered as having at least three dimensions—a sensory-spatial dimension, an existential dimension and a valuative dimension. The sensory-spatial is meant to represent the perceptions related to body conformation, spatial position, etc. (cf. body orientation). The existential aspect is suggested to represent the perceptions pertaining to substantiveness, realness and vulnerability (cf. body boundaries). The perceptions constituting the proposed valuative dimension are those concerned with the value of the body's appearance and function (cf. body cathexis and body type).

Concluding comment

It is, of course, appreciated that the foregoing review and commentary has been selective and in many ways necessarily superficial. It is more indicative of possibilities than substantive of applied findings. But if I am right, research in this area of our work has just reached the threshold of precision and before we cross it to more rewarding findings we will need a more sophisticated vision of both methods and theory.

Note

1 This is a revised text of a lecture given at the University of London Institute of Education in the series 'New Directions in Movement Studies', 1973.

References

Allport, G. (1963), *Pattern and Growth in Personality*, New York, Holt, Rinehart.

Antonelli, S. (ed.) (1966), *Proceedings of 1st International Congress of Sport Psychology*, Psicologia dello Sport, Rome, FMSI.

Atkinson, J. W. (1964), *An Introduction to Motivation*, New Jersey, Van Nostrand.

Atkinson, J. W. and Feather, N. (1966), *A Theory of Achievement Motivation*, New York, Wiley.

Bardwick, J. (1971), *Psychology of Women*, New York, Harper & Row.

Beisser, A. (1967), *The Madness in Sports*, New York, Appleton-Century-Crofts.

Berlin, P. (1972), 'Hypothesized Motives for Women's Involvement in Sports', Lecture, University of Massachusetts.

Broadbent, D. E. (1958), *Perception and Communication*, London, Pergamon Press.

Broadbent, D. E. (1971), *Decision and Stress*, London, Academic Press.

Cattell, R. B. (1965), *The Scientific Analysis of Personality*, Harmondsworth, Penguin.

Cofer, C. and Johnson, W. (1960), 'Personality Dynamics in Relation to Exercise and Sport', in *Science and Medicine of Exercise and Sport*, New York, Harper.

Cratty, B. J. (1972), *Physical Expressions of Intelligence*, New Jersey, Prentice-Hall.

Dember, W. (1970), *General Psychology—Modelling Behaviour and Experience*, New Jersey, Prentice-Hall.

Dember, W. and Earl, R. (1957), 'Analysis of Exploratory, Manipulatory and Curiosity Behaviours', *Psychological Review*, 64.

Duffy, E. (1962), *Activation and Behaviour,* New York, Wiley.

Earl, R. (1961), *A Theory of Stimulus Selection*, California, Hughes Ground.

Eysenck, H. J. (1965), *Facts and Fiction in Psychology,* Harmondsworth, Penguin.

Feather, N. (1967), 'Valence of Outcomes and Expectation of Success in Relation to Task Difficulty and Perceived Locus of Control', *Journal of Personal and Social Psychology*, 7.

Fisher, S. and Cleveland, S. E. (1958), *Body Image and Personality*, New Jersey, Van Nostrand.

Fleishman, E. (1964), *The Structure and Measurement of Physical Fitness,* New Jersey, Prentice-Hall.

Gagne, R. and Fleishman, E. (1959), *Psychology and Human Performance*, New York, Holt, Rinehart.

Helson, H. (1959), 'Adaptation Level Theory' in Koch (ed.), *Psychology: a Study of Science*, Vol. 1, New York, McGraw-Hill.

Humphrey, J. H. (1973), *Teaching Slow Learners Through Active Games*, Springfield, Ill., Thomas.

Ismail, A. H. and Gruber, J. J. (1968), *Motor Aptitude and Intellectual Performance,* Columbus, Ohio, Merritt.

Jones, M. (1970), 'Perception, Personality and Movement Characteristics of Women Specialist Students of Physical Education', Leicester University, unpublished thesis.

Jourard, S. M. and Secord, P. F. (1954), 'Body Size and Body Cathexis', *Journal of Consultative Psychology*, 18.

Kane, J. E. (1968), *Adult Involvement in Games*, Proceedings of ICHPER World Conference, Dublin; AAHPER, Washington.

Kane, J. E. (1971), 'Personality, Arousal and Performance', *International Journal of Sports Psychology*, 1, 3.

Kane, J. E. (1972), *Psychological Aspects of Physical Education and Sport*, London, Routledge & Kegan Paul.

Kane, J. E. (1974), *Physical Education in the Secondary School,* (Schools Council Research Studies), London, Macmillan.

Kenyon, G. S. (1970), *Contemporary Psychology of Sport*, Chicago, Athletic Institute.

Kephart, N. C. (1960), *The Slow Learner in the Classroom*, Columbus, Ohio, Merritt.

Knapp, B. (1963), *Skill in Sport*, London, Routledge & Kegan Paul.

Kroll, W. (1969), *Current Strategies and Problems in Personality Assessment of Athletes*, Proceedings of Symposium on Motor Learning, Chicago, Athletic Institute.

Lacey, J. I. (1959), 'Psycho-physiological Approaches to the Evaluation of Psycho-therapeutic Process and Outcome' in Rubenstein, E. and Parloff, M. (eds), *Research in Psychotherapy*, Washington, National Publishing Co.

Littig, L. (1967), 'Sex and Experimenter Interaction in Serial Learning', *Journal of Verbal Learning and Verbal Behaviour*, 6.

McClelland, D. (1961), *The Achieving Society*, New Jersey, Van Nostrand.
Musgrove, F. (1968), 'Curriculum Objectives', *Journal of Curriculum Studies*, 1, 1.
Ogilvie, B. and Tutko, T. (1966), *Problem Athletes and How to Handle Them*, London, Pelham.
Oliver, J. N. (1960), 'The Effects of Physical Conditioning Exercises and Activities in the Mental Characteristics of ESN Boys', *British Journal of Educational Psychology*, 28.
Oxendine, J. (1968), *Psychology of Motor Learning*, New York, Appleton-Century-Crofts.
Speilberger, C. (1966), 'Theory and Research on Anxiety', in Speilberger (ed.), *Anxiety and Behavior*, New York, Academic Press.
Tattersfield, C. R. (1971), 'Competitive Sport and Personality Development', University of Durham, unpublished thesis.
Vanek, M. and Cratty, B. J. (1970), *Psychology and the Superiorø Athlete*, New York, Macmillan.
Verhoff, J. (1969), 'Social Comparison and the Development of Achievement Motivations', in Smith (ed.), *Achievement-Related Motives in Children*, New York, Russell Sage Foundation.
Weiner, B. and Kukla, A. (1970), 'An Attributional Analysis of Achievement Motivation', *Journal of Personal and Social Psychology*, 15.
Welford, A. T. (1968), *Fundamentals of Skill*, London, Methuen.
Whiting, H. T. A. (1970), *Acquiring Ball Skill*, London, Bell.
Williams, J. *et al.* (1970), 'Personality Traits of Champion Female Fencers', *Research Quarterly*, October.
Willis, J. and Bethe, W. (1970), 'Achievement Motivation, Implications for Physical Activity', *Quest*, XIII.
Witkin, H. A. *et al.* (1962), *Psychological Differentiation*, New York, Wiley.
Wyrick, W. (1971), 'How Sex Differences affect Research in Physical Education', in D.G.W.S. Report *Women in Sport*, Washington, AAHPER.

11

New directions in the sociology of education and implications for physical education

E. Hoyle

The purpose of this paper is to outline some of the recent trends in the sociology of education and to examine their implications for the study of physical education. Clearly in a short paper these topics can be dealt with only in the most sketchy manner. In particular, the application of the newer approaches in the sociology of education to physical education is treated largely in a summary form with only one aspect—the impetus given to the study of the PE curriculum—treated in anything more than an outline manner. The paper is thus intended only to sensitise physical educationists to the newer sociological approaches and, I hope, to encourage further reading and discussion.

New directions in the sociology of education

The new directions in the sociology of education can perhaps be seen as having three major characteristics: (a) a shift in paradigm from a 'system' to an 'action' approach, (b) a growing concern with the curriculum as an object of sociological analysis, and (c) an increasing concern with the study of educational ideologies and their source. Each of these can be briefly considered in turn.

It is perhaps appropriate to consider first, and to spend most time on, the shift in paradigm—that is in the pre-theoretical notions underlying research—from a 'system' to an 'action' perspective.[1] It is argued that of the 'two sociologies', the system approach has been dominant. This paradigm takes order as the central sociological problem, and assumes that social groups have a core of central values from which are derived the norms which inform the expectations to which individuals tend to conform as they are socialised into certain social roles. The perspective thus focuses on the social system as a phenomenon external to the individual actor. It is, of course, particularly the approach of the functionalist school of sociology, and in this form the system model has been widely attacked, for example by 'conflict' theorists. But it can be argued that these attacks have themselves been mounted from within the system paradigm, that is, the debate has been about the degree of integration between institutions rather than about the meaning which institutions have for the individual. The 'action' perspective, on the other hand, treats the actions of individuals as logically more significant than 'systems' as the object of study. It emphasises individual autonomy and voluntarism, and conceptualises man as a 'meaning' giver. Thus individuals are seen as acting in accordance with their 'definition of the situation' rather than in accordance with the external constraints of the social system. The 'action' perspective is far from being new in sociology, but it has come to be strongly re-emphasised in recent years.

The sociology of education has naturally been influenced by the re-affirmation of the action perspective in sociology generally. It has led to a questioning of the earlier emphasis given in the sociology of education to roles—especially where these were conceptualised in terms of the expectations attached rather than in terms of the role-creating activity of individuals, to organisations—where these were conceptualised as entities almost independent of those who 'people' them, and to institutions—especially where there was an emphasis on the economic functions of educational institutions.

This shift in perspective implied that the sociology, including the sociology of education, should concern itself with new types of data. The shift has been from 'second order constructs', i.e. the constructs which sociologists apply to situations, to 'first order constructs', i.e. the constructs by which men make sense of their real-life situations. The new sociology is concerned with seeking to understand how men define their situation.

> The intent is to discover how members of a system perceive, delineate, define and clarify, and how they actually perform their activities. It represents an attempt to discover what meanings actors attach to their own acts. The challenge is not simply to describe social phenomena or events from an

observer's perspective, but to get inside the events to see what kind of conceptual equipment or theories the actors themselves are utilizing as they organize the phenomena of their lives (McKinney, 1970).

This approach is thus concerned with the phenomenological world of actors and is hence usually referred to as phenomenological sociology.[2] The approach clearly has implications for data collection. The summary statistics gathered by researches and various other agencies are treated with considerable suspicion because in their abstraction they distort 'reality'. The methodological approach is mainly one of observation and extended interview.[3] The purpose of the sociology of education is thus seen less as a matter for collecting data on, say, 'educational wastage' than as a procedure for understanding 'life in classrooms'.

The second trend in the sociology of education is a growing concern with the curriculum. Traditional approaches have been largely concerned with the structure of education rather than with its content. The concern with content is a strong trend in this country at the present time, with the sociologists of education at the London Institute of Education and at the Open University making the running. The approach has two points of departure: the sociology of knowledge, which treats all knowledge as the product of social groups rather than having an 'ideal' form, and phenomenological sociology which, as might be inferred from what has gone above, is concerned with the way in which knowledge is generated by actors in a social situation. Again a short paper does not provide the opportunity for considering the relationship between these components, nor their antecedents in the history of sociology.[4] Leaving aside the phenomenological component, we can summarise the 'sociology of knowledge' component as follows. The curriculum is a social product; it should not be taken as 'given' by the sociologist of education but rather treated as 'problematic'. The sociologist is concerned to discover why a given curriculum exists at a given point in time. Moreover, the 'subjects' of the curriculum have to be treated as 'problematic'. To justify school subjects in terms of university subjects is simply to shift the problem to another level. There are no 'subjects' in the 'real' world; they are simply convenient ways of carving up reality—and to some extent creating orders of meaning. These ways are relative to particular societies and their cultures at particular points in time.

(One can illustrate this by reference to sociology itself. Although going strong at the moment it is a relatively new 'subject', but of course the subject matter of sociology has existed as long as the existence of human groups.) Many subjects now being taught are relatively new as 'subjects'. These subjects, and their relative place in an academic hierarchy, are social products. They emphasise only certain ways of ordering knowledge and indeed they emphasise a preference for certain 'ways of knowing' over others. And importantly they also serve to create a gap between 'academic knowledge' and 'everyday knowledge' even though each is concerned with the same world.

The study of the curriculum can proceed at different levels. One can perhaps very generally identify three. Moving from the micro to the macro, one can begin with the phenomenological level. Here the investigator observes the interaction between teachers and pupils to determine how, at the classroom level, the teacher conveys the message of which knowledge is 'worthwhile' and how pupils react to this message (see Keddie, 1971). This procedure can also be applied to the school staff as a whole, and the basis on which the curriculum is determined can be inferred from the activities of head and staff. The second level we can refer to as the professional level. This involves an examination of the profession as a whole, and such sub-professions as physical education within it, in order to establish what role it plays in determining the curriculum. The approach is not here phenomenological but involves the analysis of the professional literature, conference agendas, the role of the training institutions, the functioning of subject associations as pressure groups, etc. Methodology would involve, for example, content analysis of the various forms of documentation. Or it may involve a study of individuals as they pass through their professional careers to determine what influences bear on the way in which they implement the curriculum.[5] Finally, there is the societal level, at which one is concerned to disentangle the influence of social, political, economic, cultural and other factors upon the curriculum—or upon a subject within it—at a given point in time or over time. In fact, physical education is in a strong position in this regard, since it has been the object of more competent historical analysis than many other school subjects, and its historians have, on the whole, tended to be sensitive to social influences. Yet there is obviously much more interesting work to be done here by investigators who are both historically and sociologically informed.

This point takes us to the third of our three trends in the sociology of education, that is, the study of ideological factors which help to shape the structure and content of education. This is far from being a new departure and was, indeed, a central concern for two of the pioneers of the sociology of education, Durkheim and Mannheim. It has nevertheless been underplayed in the development of the subject, which has tended to take structure, rather than the ideologies which have generated that structure, as a major focus of concern. This focus is now in the process of being revived.[6] Educational theories, whether explicit or implicit, in discussions about, for example, secondary organisation, are treated as necessarily partial perspectives which are relative to particular groups which are seeking either to legitimate the control which they have or, in other cases, to attain influence over the educational system and its content either in whole or in part. It follows from what has gone before that current sociological interest is with the influence of ideology on the curriculum. The methodology is largely a matter of the analysis of public statements and literature emanating from various groups over a period of time and through a study of reports of educational practice, attempting to assess the impact of various ideologies. This has reference to physical education in so far as ideologies of education give greater or lesser weight to its physical aspects, and more generally to its socialising and aesthetic components.

These, then, are three broad trends which can be identified in the sociology of education and to which physical education can with profit give some attention. The three trends tend to be linked by those who would give the sociology of education a new direction, but they need not necessarily be linked together. Although it is possible to link phenomenological studies with studies of ideology, this has been achieved to a lesser degree than is currently assumed. That is, studies of the curriculum and of educational ideologies can proceed without any reference to the phenomenological perspective in education. The view of the present author is that whilst the phenomenological approach has brought fresh insights to the study of social phenomena, it is not to be seen as being equated with sociology as a whole. It is the present author's view that sociology still has a need to generalise, however unsatisfactory its data might be, and that the content of sociology is not exhausted by a consideration of the personal encounter or of the everyday conceptualising activities of men. In spite of the enormous difficulties involved in reconciling the two sociologies, there is no overwhelming case for taking an exclusive position.[7] The 'new' sociology of education is very much concerned with 'demystifying' education and particularly the curriculum, but there is the danger that this approach can itself generate new 'mystification'. Nor should it be thought that the newer sociologists in criticising the 'values' of others are themselves value-free. By their own logic they cannot be since their own 'knowledge' is just as much a social product as that of others. Finally, the fact that much of the new sociology of education is concerned with 'demystifying' the curriculum and the teaching relationship raises a pedagogical problem for the teacher-trainer. It is no bad thing to encourage in students a critical stance towards their subject, but teacher training is also about commitment. The balance between criticism and commitment is now easy to achieve, and perhaps the new approach to sociology of education makes commitment all that much more difficult to achieve if its 'demystification' becomes a 'debunking' exercise. Yet in spite of these difficulties, the new approach has a very positive contribution to make to research, to theory development, and to teacher-training.

Application to physical education

It is not possible in a short paper to structure the field for the application of the newer sociological approaches to physical education—even if the author was capable of doing this, which is not the case. All that can be done is to explore some possibilities in one area. The area chosen is the middle one of the three discussed above, i.e. the sociological approach to the study of the curriculum. More specifically we will be concerned with PE as part of the school curriculum and with the sorts of question which might be asked in future research on the curriculum. The other two approaches, and especially the phenomenological approach, will not, however, be entirely neglected.

The focus will be on PE as a subject in the curriculum, and consideration will be given to three aspects: content, pedagogy and evaluation.[8] These can be considered in turn.

Content

The new approach in the sociology of the curriculum demands that each existing subject should be treated as 'problematic'. That is, its existence should not be taken for granted, but the reasons for its existence should be scrutinised. Thus physical education is to be treated as problematic. As a matter of fact this has been an approach taken by some eminent theorists. For example, in a recent book Munrow (1972) writes: 'There is some validity in regarding physical education less as a school subject than as an area of education embracing a number of separate subjects. . . .' However, the insights of the physical education theorist tend to be based on general experience and reflection on it, rather than on research of the kind currently advocated by the newer sociologists. The latter would allow their theories to emerge from their data, and their data would be the working assumptions about physical education—about its aims, scope, content, boundaries, etc.—which PE teachers hold and which guide their daily activities. However, we have as yet no published body of research of this kind, nor have the sociologists of the curriculum necessarily waited for the phenomenological data before commenting on the content of various subjects. So we can perhaps follow this lead and suggest some of the questions which might be asked—and also indulge in some speculation.

If we are treating the subject as problematical we can ask whether physical education is any more than what teachers labelled as physical educationists actually *do*. Is there a core of skills and knowledge (using knowledge in a broad sense which is not necessarily cognitive) which constitutes an identifiable subject matter of something that is termed 'physical education'? Some look for a 'core' content based on human movement. Others see physical education as an aggregation of activities involving physical skills. It perhaps follows from Munrow's view of physical education referred to above that he should take this view. He identifies ten categories of skill: gravity, friction, throwing, strutting, pulling/pushing, lifting, swimming, combat; moving ball games; tactical games, manipulative (e.g. sailing, gliding), and deliberative (e.g. camping, canoeing). This is a useful taxonomy as far as it goes, but as Munrow points out, some activities, e.g. rock climbing, rifle shooting, archery are not so easily placed. Moreover, an approach to PE which takes skill as a central concept excludes other curriculum-relevant factors such as context and values (aesthetic, competitive, utilitarian) which might be more central to other theorists of physical education. Mauldon (1970) illustrates the dilemma of the physical educationist. She writes: 'I decided that any attempt to answer my original question "What is PE?" was doomed to failure—it is no one thing—it would seem to possess a certain quality of flexibility that enables it to be bent and twisted to mean all things to all men—and women.' Where this would be accepted by the sociologist as a very interesting departure point for the study of the PE curriculum, the situation is naturally perceived by the physical educationist as a situation of dissonance and as indicating a need to re-affirm certain positive principles. Thus Mauldon continues: 'My course of action from here was now clear—I must move from *description* to *prescription*—from what *is* to what *should be*.'

A sociologist of the curriculum studying PE would bring to bear the concepts which are being generally developed within the sociology of the curriculum, take a particular focus and see PE in a wider curriculum context. For example, it might be profitable to use the concept of boundary as a means of focusing on the nature of physical education. This would enable him to relate PE to other parts of the curriculum and to perceive PE dynamically. It is fair to say that recent trends in education can be seen in terms of the growing permeability of boundaries—between subjects, between teachers at the level of their daily work, between teachers and pupils in terms of control, between school and community, etc, etc. In a word, there is a shift from closed to open systems.[9]

Taking such a focus one could examine a number of boundaries and raise quite crucial questions. With reference to boundaries within physical education one could explore whether there is a 'core' or whether there are quite distinctive components of what is classified as physical education, with little evidence of their weakening. This could also take account of the values pervading different physical activities, e.g. whether there is a distinctive boundary between aesthetic and competitive values. With reference to boundaries between PE and other components of the curriculum, one could investigate whether stronger boundaries existed between the different components of physical education than between some components of physical education and some other subjects. For example, the boundary between dance and outdoor activities could be stronger than that between dance and drama, English or art, and stronger than the boundary between outdoor pursuits, geography and biology. Finally, one perhaps should consider the strength of the boundary between physical education and institutionalised physical activities outside the school. For example, if a large school employs specialist outside coaches for games, then the boundary between a particular game and some other part of the PE curriculum, say educational gymnastics, is likely to be stronger than the boundary between in-school swimming and out-of-school swimming.

Perhaps some of the basic questions to be asked are as follows. Is physical education centrifugal or centripetal, that is, are we seeing a diversification which is breaking down the boundary around the subject so that it is to some degree losing its identity, or is a central core emerging which will become salient in all areas of physical activity? Or indeed, are both processes to some degree at work—if this is not a paradox? This question can be asked of physical education as a school subject and also of physical education as a theoretical study. (This paper has largely taken the former as a central focus.) If it is accepted that the values pervading physical education are moving from extrinsic utilitarian values to intrinsic non-utilitarian values in which self-actualisation—or whatever we choose to call it—informs curriculum objectives, does this intrinsic element generate centripetality because self-actualisation implies choice and hence a range of activities to choose from? Of course these are questions with which physical educationists are very much concerned.[10] The sociologist would seek answers to these questions at the different levels of analysis mentioned above through studying institutions, documentary analysis, and via questionnaires and interviews. But a phenomenological sociologist would in particular seek to ascertain through detailed observation of the behaviour of physical education teachers what were their working assumptions regarding the nature of physical education and its content. A sociologist of this persuasion would make the valid point that it is not sufficient to study affirmations made about physical education by the professional elite since there is inevitably a considerable gap between theory and practice. The phenomenological sociologist is interested in the 'real' world of the physical education teacher.

Pedagogy

Much of what has just been said above regarding the identification of the content of physical education at the level of the practitioner applies *a fortiori* to the study of pedagogy. Esland (1971) groups questions which might sensitise the researcher in this field under three headings: assumptions about learning, about the child's intellectual status, and about teaching style. Although the questions cited as examples mainly relate to the cognitive domain, they could be suggestive for students of physical education. Examples of pertinent questions relative to PE taking the three Esland headings might be as follows:

Assumptions about learning

(a) What theory of skill acquisition—implicit or explicit—is dominant?
(b) What assumptions are made about the differentiation of pupils according to perceived physical abilities?
(c) To what extent is interest taken as a major motivation in acquiring a skill?
(d) Is motivation made relevant 'for the present' or 'for the future'?

Assumptions about the child's status as a physical performer

(a) Does implicit or explicit somatotyping occur—in general terms?
(b) Does somatotyping occur in relation to specific activities?
(c) What assumptions are made about the child's physical status in relation to: sex, social class, intellectual status in the school, social status in the school?[11]

Assumptions about teaching style

(a) Is the approach problem-solving or didactic?
(b) Is competition emphasised in physical activities?
(c) Have pupils a high or low control over choice of physical activities?
(d) To what degree are pupils expected to 'intellectualise' physical activity?

Evaluation

Perhaps enough has already been said above to indicate the sort of question which the sociologist might raise in relation to evaluation. Examples are:

(a) How does the teacher assess a 'good' performance in a physical activity?
(b) Are clear pass/fail criteria used?

(c) What is regarded as achievement in physical education as a whole?
(d) Are children evaluated against each other or against their own previous performance?
(e) What use is made of marks, grades, standards, etc.?
(f) Is physical education an examination subject?

Again these are questions which are very much exercising physical educationists at the present time. They can be approached at several levels, but again it should be said that the newer sociology strongly advocates detailed case studies of behaviour in physical education settings. This brings the sociologist face to face with 'reality' as opposed to the non-reality which phenomenological sociologists ascribe to summary data and statistics. At the same time the method clearly has considerable inherent problems of its own: the non-generalisability of case studies, the idiosyncratic inferences drawn by individual observers, the ultimate need for categorisation. On the last point, it will be clear to the reader that there will be variations in assumptions about content, pedagogy and evaluation not only on an individual basis but also on a category basis (e.g. sex, age, type of training). If traditional sociology is guilty of reifying such categories, then perhaps phenomenological sociology could be in danger of undervaluing them.

Conclusion

In a short paper such as this, one can only give the briefest of outlines of current trends in sociology. In consequence, the account considerably oversimplifies what is quite a complex set of issues. One can only hope that the interested reader will pursue some of the references given in order to obtain a better picture of the current trends. As to the application of the newer approaches to the sociological study of the curriculum to the case of physical education, there exists something of a paradox which has already been hinted at in this paper. The questioning stance which is necessary in such studies might not be so readily assumed by a physical educationist who naturally, in the last analysis, has a strong commitment to his subject, and in any case will almost inevitably have a distinctive set of values *vis-à-vis* PE. On the other hand, the sociologist without such experience of the world of physical education, without a considerable period of immersion in the field, would perhaps be unable to pick up the full meaning of behaviour in physical education contexts. The present writer, as someone outside the PE profession, is very conscious of his ignorance about the current state of physical education. There is no obvious solution to this dilemma.

Notes

1 See Dawe (1970) for a valuable analysis of the two approaches.

2 Some of the major protagonists are Schutz, Berger, Douglas, Cicourel and Garfinkel (who coined the term ethnomethodology to describe his mode of understanding the taken-for-grantedness of reality). The work of Goffman, Becker and others is also relevant. It is impossible to identify the different strands within this general movement, nor consider the relationship between them in a short paper. The interested reader should consult Filmer *et al.* (1972) and Douglas (1971) or, for a briefer statement, Esland (1971).

3 For an application of the method to a British school situation, see Keddie (1971).

4 See Berger and Luckmann (1967) for an account. Also relevant to the whole of this paper are the units in Course E 282—*School and Society*—of the Open University.

5 Forthcoming data of this sort will be provided by the Schools Council study of the PE curriculum carried out by John Kane and June Layson and by a study carried out amongst PE teachers in a northern city by Eric Ward (I. M. Marsh College) and Kevin Hardman (Liverpool University).

6 See, for example, the recent book of readings edited by Hopper (1971).

7 See B. Bernstein's Unit 17 in the Open University Course E 282—*School and Society*—for an excellent balanced review of the state of the sociology of education.

8 This approach has much in common with that of Esland (1971) who suggests a framework of *pedagogical perspective, subject perspective* and *career perspective*. His first two categories are here reversed and *content* is substituted as an alternative to the broader concept of *subject* which here includes content and pedagogy, with *evaluation* being added. The *career* approach is a useful one but the present author sees it as conceptually distinct, and, although it is very important, he will not have the opportunity of developing it in this paper.

9 In this context see Bernstein's two highly perceptive articles on 'open schools' (Bernstein, 1967) and on 'classification and frame' (Bernstein, 1971).

10 And not only physical educationists. See a recent article by Robin Marlar, 'School Sport—What gives now?', *Sunday Times*, 31 December 1972. The following will give a flavour of the article:

> The fact is that the traditional framework of physical education has got the worm in it: and no physical educationalist can prove that the increased freedom to choose, the increased facilities even, are being accompanied by an increase in effective supervision. Without this the self-discipline and the collective discipline inherent in any form of useful physical education gives way to the characteristics of the rabble. . . . Until we find out just how far out of balance is our education between mental and physical let us propose this interim measure: that no headmaster be appointed by local authority or governing body unless he can satisfy his assessors—by his record—of a commitment to physical education in general, and team games in particular, for children all the way from 8 to 18.

11 This area provides a neat example of what the new sociology is attempting. We know from existing studies (e.g. McIntosh, 1966; Start, 1966) that there is a close relationship between stream and representation in school teams. The sociologist of education is now enjoined to study the process which yields this statistically demonstrated relationship. A hint of the factors at work here is given in Hargreaves (1968).

References

Berger, P. L. and Luckmann, T. (1967), *The Social Construction of Reality*, London, Allen Lane, the Penguin Press.
Bernstein, B. (1967), 'Open schools, open society?', *New Society*, 14 September 1967.
Bernstein, B. (1971), 'On the classification and framing of knowledge', in Young, M. F. D. (1971).
Dawe, A. (1970), 'The two sociologies', *Brit. J. Soc.* 21(2).
Douglas, J. (1971), *Understanding Everyday Life*, London, Routledge & Kegan Paul.
Esland, G. M. (1971), 'Teaching and learning as the organization of knowledge', in Young, M. F. D. (1971).
Filmer, P., Philipson, M., Silverman, D. and Walsh, D. (1972), *New Directions in Sociological Theory*, London, Macmillan.
Hargreaves, D. H. (1968), *Social Relations in a Secondary School*, London, Routledge & Kegan Paul.
Hopper, E. (1971), *Readings in the Theory of Educational Systems*, London, Hutchinson.
Keddy, N. (1971), 'Classroom knowledge' in Young (1971).
McIntosh, P. C. (1966), 'Mental ability and success in school sport', *Res. Phys. Ed.* 1.
McKinney, J. L. (1969), 'Typification, typologies and sociological theory', *Social Forces*, 48(1).
Mauldon, B. (1970), 'What is Physical Education?', *Bull. Physical Ed.* 8(3), July.
Munrow, A. D. (1972), *Physical Education: a Discussion of Principles*, London, Bell.

Start, K. B. (1966), 'Substitution of games performance for academic achievements as a means of achieving status among secondary school children', *Brit. J. Soc.* 17(3).
Young, M. F. D. (1971), *Knowledge and Control: New Directions in the Sociology of Education*, London, Collier-Macmillan.

12

Exercise, health and fitness—the teacher's responsibility

Dudley F. Cooper

In the Schools Council Research Study *Physical Education in the Secondary School*, Kane (1974) reviewed over 200 publications to establish the objectives of physical education most frequently mentioned. Nine objectives were finally tabulated and were ranked in order of importance by nearly 900 teachers of physical education as follows.

1 Motor skills
2 Self-realisation
3 Leisure
4 Emotional stability
5 Moral development
6 Social competence
7 Organic development
8 Cognitive development
9 Aesthetic appreciation

From this study it would appear that the general and traditional view that physical education is 'all about physical fitness' is not held by modern teachers. This probably reflects current psychosocial bias in educational thought, but it could mean also that teachers are not convinced that organic development and fitness are objectives worth pursuing independently from other objectives.

Although, historically, this represents a major change in the attitude of teachers, no equivalent change has occurred with physicians and others concerned primarily with health and development. Indeed it would be true to say that there has been a significant move in the direction of a more enthusiastic embracement of the theory that regular physical activity is an important factor in the maintenance of good health. This fact is quite remarkable, for in recent years there has been substantial critical review of the literature devoted to exercise, longevity and health including criticism of such classical studies as those of Morris (1959), on bus conductors, bus drivers and coronary heart disease. Most of the problems seem to be associated with the difficulties experienced by all workers in the area, namely the apparently impossible tasks of isolating the exercise factor and of obtaining perfectly matched groups. Many like Astrand (1954) and Fox and Skinner (1964), however, are convinced enough by the considerable indirect and anecdotal evidence to advocate strongly that fitness training should be given the highest priority both as a prophylactic measure and in rehabilitation. Such a view need not be incompatible, moreover, with the opinions of the teachers outlined in the first paragraph, for it merely places organic development as the basis for the realisation of the other objectives, a premise with which few outside the physical education profession would disagree.

This approach has several distinct advantages in that some of the skills needed for the job are clearly indicated, objectives are clearly defined and, moreover, these objectives may be attained and the effectiveness of the whole programme evaluated. To many teachers, however, evaluation suggests a scientific approach which they find inhibiting, and there is no question that over the years a great deal of priceless data has been lost because of this attitude. It is the purpose of the paper, therefore, to attempt to show that evaluation is neither inhibiting nor beyond the competence of any serious-minded teacher once he has accepted his responsibility in the area of health and fitness. These responsibilities have not been spelt out for the teacher for some time, in fact probably not since formal syllabuses from the then Ministry of Education ceased to be issued, and this may account for teacher attitudes. In the hope of gaining some converts and of jogging the consciences of many others the following are suggested.

1 Development of the respiratory and cardiovascular systems.
2 Development of adequate (i.e. above minimal) levels of strength, particularly the back and abdomen.
3 Maintenance of minimal levels of flexibility.

4 Instruction in how to lie, sit, stand, walk and carry.
5 Teaching of basic theory and practice of training.
6 Inculcation of interest in regular physical exercise after the school years with explanation of the physiological, medical and psychological value.

(Adapted from Astrand and Rodahl, 1970)

It is not intended to describe here methods and the theory of training as it is assumed that knowledge of these is part and parcel of every physical education teacher's background. Instead it is proposed to outline some techniques of evaluation, for it is felt that this is the real stumbling-block to progress.

Evaluation

Evaluation can be a powerful motivator if used regularly and if results are published. Tests must be carefully chosen with regard to the age, size and sex of the subjects and results should be filed so that a complete record of a child's progress may be available even years after he/she has left school. Such data may be invaluable for longitudinal studies, especially if measurements are made in a standardised way.

Many sophisticated laboratory tests have been designed to measure fitness and the capacity for hard work, but it is accepted that such facilities will not be available to teachers in general nor will many feel competent to perform them. Consequently most will turn to such well-known test batteries as the AAHPER Youth Fitness Test (AAHPER, 1965) or the Fleishman Physical Fitness Tests (Fleishman, 1964). It should be pointed out, however, that most of the items in these test batteries are highly specific and the same tests must be used on subsequent occasions if any reliable information is to be obtained. Manuals are available for the above-mentioned tests, but for those with little experience of testing fitness the following test would make a useful starting point and has the added value of being accepted and standardised internationally (Larson, 1974).

General

Suitable for ages 6–32 years. Subjects should be healthy and well prepared for the tests. They must also fully understand the nature and purpose of the tests. It is recommended that items 1, 2 and 3 should be given on one day and items 4–6 on the next day.

1 50 metre sprint. Standing start. *Score*: Time to nearest tenth of a second. (Weather should be relatively windless without extremes of temperature.)

2 Standing long jump. A flat, non-slip surface should be used. Subject stands with toes just behind the take-off line and jumps when ready. After making a preliminary swing with the arms, he swings them forward vigorously, springing with both feet simultaneously to land as far forward as possible.

Score: Distance jumped in centimetres.

3 Distance run. Men and boys, 12 years and over 1,000 or 2,000 m.
Women and girls, 12 years and over 800 or 1,500 m.
Children under 12 years 600 m.

Distance may be run or walked if necessary. *Score*: Nearest second.

4 (a) Pull-ups. Men and boys 12 years and over. A horizontal bar 2–5 cm in diameter is used. The bar should be set so that even the tallest subject will be vertically suspended. Subject stands on a stool, grasps bar in overgrasp (palms facing forward), hands shoulder width apart. At the signal 'Go' the subject flexes his arms and raises his body until his chin is just above the level of the bar. Without delay the body is lowered and the procedure repeated as many times as possible. *Score*: Number of times the chin is raised above the bar. Swinging is not permitted.

4 (b) Flexed arm hang. Women, girls and children under 12 years. The same bar is used as in test 4 (a). The subject stands on a stool or chair and the bar is adjusted so that when the support is removed the subject can hang with her chin above the bar, arms flexed. The subject attempts to remain in this position for as long as possible. *Score*: Time in seconds.

5 Shuttle run. A flat course of 10 m measured between two parallel base lines. Behind each base line is a semicircle 50 cm radius with centre on the base line. In the far semicircle two wood blocks (5 × 5 × 5 cm) are placed. Subject stands with foot behind near line, runs to the far line, picks up one block which he places in the start semicircle when he returns.

He then sprints to repeat the procedure with the second block. *Score*: Time to nearest tenth of a second when the second block is grounded in the circle.

6 30-second sit-ups. Subject lies on back on a mat or flat surface, feet about 30 cm apart and knees flexed at a right angle. Hands with fingers interlocked are placed behind the neck. A partner holds the subject's feet in contact with the mat or floor. On signal 'Go' the subject sits up to touch the knees with his elbows. Without pause he returns to his starting position and immediately sits up again. *Score*: Number of sit-ups completed in 30 seconds.

When the data have been collected they should be published, privately if preferred, and the scores compared with national norms. Unfortunately there are very few published norms for British school children and teachers are advised to construct their own tables, perhaps in co-operation with colleagues in other schools. It could even be a project organised by the Physical Education Inspector for the area. Where such co-operation is not possible teachers will have to rely on their own table built up over several years and based on the fact that a gradual improvement in scores will be expected as the children get older, with a plateau at the higher age-levels for those who merely wish to maintain fitness levels achieved earlier.

In addition to the above tests it is assumed that all teachers will regularly monitor the height and weight of their pupils and that they will observe their changing body proportions. Such simple observations can be exceptionally useful in the assessment of the achievements of individual children and may even be used as an aid to guidance in the selection of activities of the children.

Those seeking rather more sophisticated tests of physical work capacity will find Astrand and Rodahl's *Textbook of Work Physiology* particularly useful as an introduction to the area and will soon discover which test suits their purpose and facilities, but those who seek even simpler methods will be heartened by the growing opinion that regular tests such as running round the games field may yield quite valid assessments of the functional state of individuals. The important thing is that these tests should be undertaken, for if children see fitness as an important part of their physical education we may be some way along the road to encouraging them to make it a lifelong habit, and by so doing ensure that the more esoteric of our objectives have a chance of being attained.

References

American Association of Health, Physical Education and Recreation (1965), *AAHPER Fitness Test Manual* (rev. ed.), Washington, D.C.

Astrand, P.-O. (1954), *Experimental studies of physical working capacity in relation to sex and age*, Copenhagen, Munksgaard.

Astrand, P.-O. and Rodahl, K. (1970), *Textbook of Work Physiology*, Chicago, McGraw-Hill.

Fleishman, E. A. (1964), *The Structure and Measurement of Physical Fitness*, Englewood Cliffs, N.J., Prentice-Hall.

Fox, S. M. and Skinner, J. (1964), 'Physical activity and cardiovascular health', *Am. J. Cardiol.* 14, 731.

Kane, J. E. (1974), *Physical Education in the Secondary School* (Schools Council Research Studies), London, Macmillan.

Larson, L. A. (ed.) (1974), *Fitness, Health and Work Capacity: International Standards for Assessment,* New York, Macmillan.

Morris, J. N. (1959), 'Occupation and coronary heart disease', *Arch. Intern. Med. (Chicago)*, 104, 903.

Part 4

The Curriculum

13

Curriculum planning and development

Gordon Underwood

One of the most important tasks undertaken by the physical education teacher in a school is to plan an effective programme of work. This should involve him in a consideration of the aims and objectives of the subject, the teaching and learning experiences he wishes to give to the children, a selection of the subject matter, and the internal organisation of the school, together with some form of evaluation. It is not an easy task to plan and organise such important areas in a logical manner. The study of the curriculum is quite a recent development and many teachers have not had the opportunity to study this area in depth. Taylor (1970), in a book entitled *How Teachers Plan Their Courses*, suggested that teachers have a rather unsystematic approach to planning. However, there is little doubt that some excellent teaching is taking place in many schools, based upon the limited experience of one or a small number of teachers. The purpose of this article is to examine the main components of curriculum planning and consider their relationship.

Many alternative models have been proposed over the years, but one which has particular relevance to physical education is the model used at Sussex University for the analysis of curriculum materials.

As can be seen from Figure 13.1, the aims of the subject underpin the whole of the curriculum strategy and only this aspect is given some order of priority. This is in contrast to the school of thought known as rational curriculum planning, where the aims

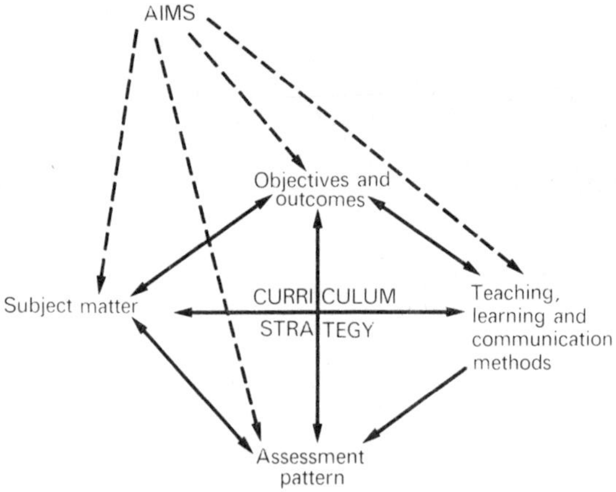

Figure 13.1 Curriculum model

and objectives are stated first and this is followed by a consideration of the teaching methods and learning experiences along with a selection of subject matter. At the end of a course an evaluation takes place, and the results should give an indication of whether or not the original objectives have been achieved.

In a review of over 200 publications, Kane (1974) suggested that there were nine main aims that are regularly found in the physical education literature. These range from the overt areas of motor skills and organic development to the more covert areas of moral development and self-realisation. The distinction made between overt or easily observed behaviours and covert or hidden attitudes may be important, as teachers find it very much easier to specify objectives in the overt areas and have less difficulty in making an evaluation at the end of the course. Whichever model of the curriculum is used, the aims of the subject are fundamental. One of the strengths of the Sussex model is that alternative routes are available in addition to the 'rational planning'. If, for example, a selection is made from the content of physical education such as swimming, this will obviously have an effect on the kinds of objectives that can be realised as well as upon the learning procedures and methods of evaluation.

There has been considerable debate about the necessity of breaking down the aims into smaller components or objectives. These would give a detailed description of the kind of behaviour that the teacher was aiming for. Bloom *et al.* (1956) made a classification of educational objectives under three main areas: the cognitive (intellectual area), the affective (emotional area) and the psychomotor (physical skills area). The objectives are arranged in hierarchical order and may be used as a useful guide, but it must be remembered that in the learning of physical skills it is impossible to isolate this from the knowledge that is being acquired and the attitudes that are being formed. In a positive attempt to help teachers formulate objectives, Taba (1962) suggested the following six criteria.

1 To describe the kind of behaviour expected and the context to which that behaviour applies.
2 To state objectives analytically and specifically.
3 To make clear distinctions among learning experiences required to attain different behaviours.
4 To ensure objectives are developmental, representing roads to travel rather than terminal points.
5 To be realistic and include only what is practicable.
6 To be broad enough to encompass all types of outcomes for which school is responsible.

It is not an easy task to specify objectives, but there can be no doubt that when this is done it gives guidance and direction to the planning of future work. It should also ensure that there is some form of logical progression. In the overt areas, such as trampolining and athletics, it is far easier to specify objectives and measure improved performance than it is in areas concerned with moral and social development. As a result, there may well be a tendency to emphasise the overt areas to the neglect of the covert and affective areas of the subject. The model also refers to 'Outcomes' which may well be unintended and cannot be specifically stated. Eisner (1969) also made this distinction when he referred to instructional objectives which specify the particular behaviour to be acquired, and expressive objectives which do not pre-specify and are classed as an 'educational encounter'. Outcomes arise from the teacher structuring situations into which children are allowed to place a personal interpretation, and this will vary with each individual. There can be no doubt that there are many valid experiences in physical education that come into this category.

The methods of communication used by the teacher to achieve

ends will differ with each individual. This will reflect his philosophy of education as well as the needs of the children e subject material. Several different teaching styles are used sical education, and these vary from pure directed teaching to a guided discovery or creative approach. The style that is adopted will change according to the nature of the subject and the stage of development. In the teaching of gymnastic skills a very directed approach may be considered to be the most effective. At a later stage, when ideas on interpretation are required, a guided discovery method may be thought to be more appropriate. Whichever methodology is used, there is no doubt that we need to gain more insight into their advantages and disadvantages. In many instances, there may be a discrepancy between the stated objectives and those that are actually achieved. There have been many methods used for studying and analysing teaching behaviour. The most prominent researcher in the field of interaction analysis has been Flanders (1970), but his categories were mainly concerned with verbal behaviour. Research work is in progress to record objectively the behaviour of both teacher and children every few seconds in a variety of physical education settings. In spite of the limitations with this type of analysis, when it is combined with videotape recording, which allows teaching situations to be played back many times, it enables the teacher to learn about himself and his teaching style. Hopefully, it will lead to improvements in teaching ability and understanding.

The subject matter of physical education in the secondary schools will usually be a selection from the six main areas of athletics, dance, games, gymnastics, swimming and outdoor pursuits. Normally a basic core from the chosen areas is followed for the first three years. This gives a firm basis from which children can make informed choices when options are offered. One of the dangers of the subject is that there is too much width and not enough depth, and that children never realise their potential in any one activity because there is not enough time devoted to achieving quality performance. Most teachers allow children to choose at some stage in the curriculum, but perhaps initially this needs to be a guided choice by categorising activities, for example, into indoor and outdoor or individual and team. Selection is then made from the categories offered, which ensures both width and depth.

Changes in human behaviour do take time in which to develop. An essential of any planning is that experiences build upon each other and that the continuity is realised by the children. This can happen in two ways. First in a vertical fashion within the subject, where work in one term or year is built on in the future, and second in a horizontal manner, where links are made with other aspects of physical education or perhaps even with other subjects in the curriculum. The Schools Council Enquiry into *Physical Education in Secondary Schools* carried out by Kane (1974) indicated that nearly two-thirds of the departments were involved in inter-disciplinary studies to some extent. This suggests that a great deal of collaboration is taking place between departments in the schools. However, the exact format of these integrated studies is not specified. The Keele Integrated Studies Project (1973) defined integration as 'the exploration of any large area, theme, or problem which (a) requires the help of more than one subject discipline for its full understanding, and (b) is best taught by the concerted action of a team of teachers'. There are many topic areas that could well be investigated in this way. For example, 'Sport and Society' could lead to a study of the many aspects of sport and recreation both in the local area and society at large, whilst 'Mechanics of Movement' would inevitably link science and physics with a variety of running, striking, throwing and jumping activities.

The assessment pattern takes place at every stage in the educational process, and it is quite wrong to think of it only taking place at the end. Wilhelms (1971) referred to evaluation as feedback, and suggested that 'it resonates back through every stage of the educational process'. Evaluation is concerned with making judgments and should help in the making of future decisions. Wilhelms went on to suggest that any system of evaluation must meet some basic criteria, and four of these are particularly appropriate to physical education. The first is that it should facilitate self-evaluation. This is concerned with the learner being able to assess his own ability and potential in a variety of physical situations and being able to build positive self concepts. Second, it should encompass every objective valued by the school. This is not only in physical prowess but also in terms of knowledge and attitudes. Third, it must facilitate learning and teaching. Every aspect of evaluative information should give an indication of the effectiveness of present work and a guide to future planning. Lastly, it must produce appropriate records for every child. This should not only be a record of achievement in school teams by the more able, but also it should make reference to their attitude, contribution and personal development. Much of our evaluation can take place through simple measurement, but more sophisticated methods are also required. The triangulation method of the Ford Teaching Project (1975), where three accounts of the same lesson by the teacher, the children and an observer are elicited independently and cross-reference made, could be a rewarding area of investigation. Assessment patterns are so much easier in the more precise areas of motor performance. However, this should not prevent us from trying to achieve accurate evaluation in the less precise areas such as aesthetic appreciation.

Whatever limitations curriculum planning might have, the relationship between the main components is important if logical development is to take place. The Schools Council Physical Education Enquiry suggested that teachers would welcome help and advice in formulating objectives, planning content, selecting methods and making evaluations. There is a need to identify those departments where excellent teaching takes place, and isolate the criteria for 'good practice'. Curriculum planning and development is an area worthy of study not only for teachers in the schools, but also for students in colleges. It is hoped that the above discussion will provide some guidelines which teachers might find helpful in their planning of the curriculum.

Bibliography

Bloom, B. S. (ed.) (1956), *The Taxonomy of Educational Objectives. 1. Cognitive Domain*, New York, McKay.

Cope, E. (1975), 'Evaluation in physical education', *Journal of Psycho-Social Aspects*, Dunfermline College of PE, April.

Eisner, E. (1969), 'Instructional and expressive educational objectives: their formulations and use in curriculum', in W. J. Popham, *et al.* (eds), *Instructional Objectives*, AERA Monograph no. 3, Chicago, Ill., Rand McNally.

Eraut, M., Goad, L. and Smith, G. (1975), *The Analysis of Curriculum Materials*, University of Sussex Education Area, Occasional Paper no. 2.

Flanders, N. A. (1970), *Analyzing Teaching Behavior*, Chicago, Addison-Wesley.

Ford Teaching Project (1975), Centre for Applied Research in Education, University of East Anglia.

Golby, M., Greenwald, J. and West, R. (eds) (1975), *Curriculum Design*, London, Croom Helm.

Hooper, R. (ed.) (1971), *The Curriculum: Context, Design and Development*, Edinburgh, Oliver & Boyd.

Kane, J. E. (1974), *Physical Education in the Secondary School* (Schools

Council Research Studies), London, Macmillan.
Keele Integrated Studies Project (1973), *Schools Council Integrated Studies*, Oxford University Press for the Schools Council.
Lawton, D. (1973), *Social Change, Educational Theory and Curriculum Planning*, University of London Press.
Nicholls, A. and H. (1972), *Developing a Curriculum: A Practical Guide*, London, Allen & Unwin.
Paisley, H. A. G. (1975), *The Behavioural Strategy of Teachers*, NFER.
Pring, R. (1972), 'Aims and Objectives', in *Curriculum Philosophy and Design*, Open University E 283, Unit 7.
Pring, R. (1973), 'Objectives and innovation: the irrelevance of theory', *London Educational Review*, vol. 2, no. 3.
Richmond, W. K. (1971), *The School Curriculum*, London, Methuen.
Singer, R. N. (1974), 'A Systems Approach to Teaching Physical Education', *Journal of Health, Physical Education and Research*, September.
Taba, H. (1962), *Curriculum Development: Theory and Practice*, New York, Harcourt Brace.
Taylor, P. H. (1970), *How Teachers Plan Their Courses*, Windsor, NFER.
Tyler, R. W. (1949), *Basic Principles of Curriculum and Instruction,* Chicago, Ill., University of Chicago Press.
Underwood, G. L. (1975), Curriculum Planning and Development in Physical Education, *Bulletin of Physical Education*, vol. XI, no. 4.
Wheeler, D. K. (1967), *Curriculum Process*, Universitv of London Press.
Wilhelms, F. T. (1971), 'Evaluation as Feedback', in R. Hooper (ed.), *The Curriculum: Context, Design and Development*, Edinburgh, Oliver & Boyd.

14

Planning the physical education curriculum[1]

J. E. Kane

The challenge of what might be called the curriculum reform movement has come relatively late to physical education. The forces that have reshaped, for example, the science, mathematics and language curricula, have only begun to affect physical education. It is appropriate, therefore, to consider briefly some basic theoretical and practical issues of curriculum planning which will surely increasingly affect us in the structuring of school courses. It seems likely that teachers in physical education will be increasingly expected to make explicit the principles by which they plan for effective achievement. This is not to suggest that at present teachers are insensitive to the problems involved. Taylor (1970) in his recent assessment considers that teachers are probably aware of the complexities underlying the process of curriculum planning, but apparently do not in general seem to have developed a procedure for systematically taking them into account.

Many of the recent flood of publications dealing with the curriculum deal with the theory and structure of planning. Their main value is in drawing attention to fundamental assumptions about the curriculum, and this is, of course, of great importance for teachers. What seems to be missing at the moment is a systematic assessment of operational curriculum planning, beginning with an assessment of what teachers actually do. It seems essential as a first step to take into account the developed wisdom of experienced teachers before proposing elaborate and mostly unverifiable principles of curriculum planning. Of course the views of educational theorists must also be considered in the development of any systematic approach.

Taylor (1970) has suggested that there is little or no confusion about the main elements which need to be considered in curriculum planning, which are:

1 The knowledge which is to comprise the content
2 The purpose the knowledge is to serve
3 The means employed to achieve these purposes
4 The abilities, aptitudes, needs and interests of children
5 Criteria to be used for judging of success
6 Employment of these criteria in evaluation

For the purposes of considering the physical education curriculum these elements may be simply summarised into three focal areas:

1 Educational objectives
2 The teaching context
3 Evaluation

My task from this point will be to elaborate on these three areas, strengthening the argument with evidence from the Schools Council Survey of Physical Education in Secondary Schools in England and Wales (Kane, 1974), which reports on information from a 1-in-10 sample of all secondary schools, and all the physical education teachers employed in them.

Educational objectives

The educational objectives include both the general justification of the curriculum courses on educational grounds, and the specific changes in pupil behaviour that are intended. The recent emphasis (Bloom, 1956; Krathwohl, 1964; Mager, 1962) has been on the requirement to set out educational objectives in refined behavioural terms in three domains—cognitive, affective and psychomotor. Whether or not the choices and objectives are right is, of course, another matter. Mostly they are based on teachers' value judgments, as Hirst (1969) has argued forcibly. Central to this fundamental philosophising will be the teachers' view of what is educationally worthwhile in terms of the kind of adult that the child will become, and the kind of society to which he will belong. No doubt the teachers will choose in the process of clarifying and formulating their ideas to refer to appropriate educational theorists, and to the expressed interests and attitudes of the children they teach.

Some serious efforts are currently being made by individuals and groups working in physical education to list and categorise educational objectives for this area of the whole curriculum. While the guidelines for a classification of the cognitive and affective domains have been set down by Bloom and Krathwohl, tentative themes for the classification of the psychomotor (skill) domain are only beginning to appear now. Of these the proposals of Jewett (1971) and Simpson (1967) seem most likely to be both workable and effective. The main difficulty in preparing a taxonomy of the psychomotor area is the great variety of the kinds of tasks and skill which constitute it, and therefore the consequent problem of categorising observable levels or stages which have operational meaning, and are universally applicable. The categorical stages most likely to have greatest general relevance to the psychomotor domain might be:

1.0 Perception: identification, distinguishing, recognition
2.0 Set: mental, physical, emotional
3.0 Selection: intention, resolution, decision
4.0 Response: patterning, organisation, practice
5.0 Analysis and synthesis: mechanism, exploration, integration
6.0 Adaptation: refining, developing, creating

One very fine attempt at setting down the objectives of the physical education programme in behavioural terms is exemplified in the Battle Creek (Michigan) Curriculum Project, where a curriculum development team has outlined a finely reasoned curriculum structure as a first stage to testing it in the Michigan School system. We await with great interest reports of their operational findings.

The Schools Council investigation (Kane, 1974) indicated that the literature in physical education suggested numerous and often diffuse aims and objectives for the secondary school curriculum. The nine most often mentioned of these were assembled for rating by physical education teachers in England and Wales. The men teachers most highly rated the objectives of leisure pursuits, motor skills and self-realisation, and gave their lowest rating to cognitive development and aesthetic appreciation. Women teachers rated highest motor skills, self-realisation and emotional development, and gave the lowest-rated positions to cognitive development, organic development and aesthetic appreciation. There was therefore reasonable agreement between the men and women teachers as to the priority they attached to these objectives. They both also gave the middle, fifth-ranked position (of the nine) to moral development, which gives an indication of the profession's moderate commitment to this curricular objective. An analysis by age showed that younger teachers give higher priority to social objectives than their older colleagues. Interviews with the teachers revealed, however, that the consideration of precise objectives did not constitute a large part of their curriculum planning. Their major concern appeared to be the teaching context, and in particular the content and methods they used.

The teaching context

The teaching context is proposed to take in: (1) the selection and sequencing of the subject content; (2) the teaching methods and strategies to be employed; and (3) the consideration of factors which may limit the teacher's effectiveness. Of the substantial amount of evidence collected in our investigation of schools and teachers of physical education, a number of items relevant to the teaching context are selected for brief comment.

Time allocation for physical education

An index of average class time was used to compare the amount of time given each week to physical education with that given to English, mathematics, geography and history. On average, in the first year of secondary schooling English and mathematics received over 200 minutes per week compared with approximately 150 minutes for physical education and 90 minutes for history and geography. In the fifth year, however, while the allocation of time for English and mathematics was much the same as it had been in the first year, the time given to physical education had decreased to just over 100 minutes, and for history and geography had substantially increased, to about 145 minutes. Of the five subjects considered, only physical education had shown a decrease in time allocation, and the decrease was most noticeable in the fourth and fifth years, which also happen to be the years in which the first major public examination is most often held in England and Wales. I should add, however, that no evidence was collected on which a cause-and-effect relationship between the reduction of time for physical education and the incidence of public examination could be established.

Content and sequencing

With a view to assembling some notions of the content of the physical education programme a long list of activities was prepared. The teachers were asked to indicate which of the listed activities were included in their teaching programmes for each of the five years of secondary schooling. The findings showed, as expected, a gradual increase in the average number of activities which constituted the programmes, and linked with this was a gradual increase in the standard duration, indicating that the schools differed markedly in the number of activities they put into their programme in the later years. The mean increase shown in boys' schools and departments over the five years was found to be larger (9·2 to 11·4) than in girls' schools (8·6 to 9·1).

As the general trend was clear, that over the years of secondary schooling the number of activities increased, the extent of students' choice in the programme was investigated. There have been increasing signs in recent years that attempts are being made to satisfy students' interests and to cater for differences in needs and abilities by offering some choice of activities in the later years of the secondary school, and there have also been reports of some schools which have dispensed altogether with the physical education requirements.

In our survey we described three types of programmes—compulsory, compulsory with choice, and optional. We found that about 65 per cent of the schools have completely compulsory programmes in the first year, but less than 5 per cent of them had this kind of programme in the fifth year. Some 15 per cent of schools appear to have some form of optional programme working by the fifth year, which gives some indication that the physical education programme is no longer regarded as compulsory at this stage of schooling.

The emphasis on time, placed on six different aspects of the programme over the five years, showed that for both boys and girls most time was spent on team games. Various forms of gymnastics were ranked second in both cases. Swimming and athletics occupied the intermediate ranking and dance and outdoor pursuits were least emphasised.

Teaching styles

The way in which the teacher makes use or manipulates the curriculum content is an important factor to be considered in the planning and learning experiences; methods and styles of teaching vary according to teachers' preferred approaches and to the demands of different aspects of the programme. The teachers in our sample were asked to estimate how often they used teaching styles described as 'direct', 'guided discovery', 'problem solving', 'creative', and 'individualised programmes'. They were asked to rate their programme as a whole on the five (high point) scale. Guided discovery, direct and problem solving methods were rated highly, and styles described as creative and individualised programmes were rated relatively low. Some differences between the men and women teachers were observed, which indicated that the women used direct teacher-dominated methods less often than men. Whereas the men gave the highest mean rating to the style described as direct, the women rated guided discovery highest. The same trend towards the use of indirect styles was recognisable for the younger teachers (both men and women) in the sample when they were compared to the older teachers.

It was found that 94 per cent of the teachers regularly taught gymnastics of one form or other. These were asked to assess the extent to which they used five 'approaches' to the teaching of gymnastics. 'Lead-up stages', 'movement principles' and 'learning principles' are apparently used much more often than 'principles of mechanics' and 'physiological principles'. It was clearly noticeable, however, that the women and the younger teachers made greater use of movement principles in teaching gymnastics than did the men and the older teachers of both sexes.

Other factors affecting teachers' effectiveness

There are, of course, many other factors outside curriculum planning which may affect the teacher in carrying out his intentions. They may include such influencing forces as the prevailing attitudes and atmosphere in the school, the resources available and the number and diversity of the students. It may be that the teacher has no immediate control of these factors, which may have a widespread influence on planning and achievement. The teachers were asked to rate in terms of 'importance' twenty items which it was thought might constitute such influence factors. In the highest ranked positions (and therefore the most important) were items described as 'adequacy of facilities', 'timetable allocation', 'freedom to experiment' and 'timetable load'. When the responses to the items were intercorrelated a component analysis was undertaken. The purpose of this procedure was to identify and describe the major dimensions explaining the teachers' reactions to these items. The seven largest dimensions in order of size were described as follows:

1 Total work commitment
2 Diversity of students
3 Resources
4 Liberal atmosphere
5 Safety
6 Attitude of colleagues
7 Discipline

These factors may then be taken to describe major influences or issues affecting the teacher in the operation of the planned curriculum. The detailed argument of the way in which each of these factors may represent a gross limitation for the teacher is outlined in the major report.

Evaluation of the course

Increasing emphasis is being placed by theorists on the need to evaluate outcomes of courses. This requires initially the establishing of criteria by which the knowledge, skills and values which pupils are intended to acquire are to be assessed—whether by written test or objective examination, or by teacher rating. These criteria ought to be made explicit if they are to have meaning in the evaluation procedures for estimating the relative success of planned courses. If, of course, the objectives have been set out in behavioural terms the problems of evaluation are greatly simplified. In physical education the problems of evaluation in certain aspects of the programme (syllabus) present few difficulties, for example in the assessment of organic fitness, but with respect to proposed emotional, social, and aesthetic outcomes the difficulties of evaluation have hardly been faced.

On the broader front of curriculum evaluation, Taylor (1970) suggests that the following larger questions must be answered:

Was the course educationally sound?
Was the most effective selection of subject matter used?
Could it have been ordered better?
Were the teaching strategies sound?
Was assessment adequate?

Such information supplies the necessary feedback which provides for a dynamic curriculum structure sensitive to improvement, revitalisation and adaptation to changing personal and social expectations.

In the Schools Council survey the teachers were asked to consider the effects on their students of the physical education programme. This was an attempt to ascertain the teachers' perceptions of the outcomes and values of physical education. Thirty possible effects were listed and the teachers were required to rate each on a five-point scale, ranging from 'a great deal' to 'little or none'. The effects rated highest included 'enjoyment of participation', 'release from tension', 'general self-confidence' and 'general physical development'. When the teachers' responses were intercorrelated and a component analysis undertaken, it appears that the effects of the physical education programme as viewed by these teachers may be summarised in the following seven major factors which were identified:

1 Social awareness and responsibility
2 General physical development
3 Self-awareness
4 General movement ability
5 General interest in school
6 Enjoyment in physical activities
7 Cognitive judgment

It is somewhat surprising to note from this analysis that physical education teachers' perception of the most important outcome of their programmes is associated with the children's developing social awareness. If this is so, then the perceived function and role of the physical education teacher may have changed a great deal in recent years and deserves closer investigation.

Note

1 This is a revised text of a paper given at the London Conference of the International Council of Health, Physical Education and Recreation, 1972.

References

Bloom, B., *et al.* (1956), *Taxonomy of Educational Objectives: Handbook 1: The Cognitive Domain*, London, Longmans.
Hirst, P. (1969), 'The logic of the curriculum', *Journal of Curriculum Studies*, vol. 1, no. 2, 142–58.
Jewett, A., *et al.* (1971), 'Educational change through a taxonomy for writing Physical Educational Objectives', *Quest*, vol. XV.
Kane, J. E. (1974), *Physical Education in the Secondary School* (Schools Council Research Studies), London, Macmillan.
Krathwohl, D. R. *et al.* (1964), *Taxonomy of Educational Objectives: Handbook 2: The Affective Domain*, London, Longmans.
Mager, R. F. (1962), *Preparing Instructional Objectives*, Pal Alto, Fearon.
Simpson, E. (1967), 'The classification of educational objectives—psychomotor domain', *Illinois Teacher*, vol. X, no. 4.
Taylor, Philip H. (1970), *How Teachers Plan Their Courses: Studies in Curriculum Planning*, National Foundation for Educational Research in England and Wales; Margate, Eyre & Spottiswoode Ltd.

15

Examinations in human movement studies

Irene K. Glaister

Examinations are a method of evaluation. One would not deny that evaluation is essential, both to enable a teacher to estimate a pupil's attainment and progress, and to provide feedback as to the efficacy of his planning and teaching methods. But the need to formalise this evaluation into an 'external examination', to be taken by some pupils, is debatable. In the past, objections have been raised by leading members of the physical education profession for the following reasons: syllabuses would be determined by a central body without reference to the pupils or teachers concerned; they would lead to conformity of approach, stultifying experiment; special movement knowledge cannot be expressed in words or be 'marked out of ten'; they might encourage the separation of the theory from the practice; they might cause limited resources to be channelled to help the more gifted children at the expense of those less well endowed; enjoyment would be killed. It was also argued that activities brought their own reward, obviating the necessity for other awards. Paradoxically, while examinations were frowned upon, governing-body awards such as those of the Royal Life Saving Society, or the Amateur Swimming Association were generally accepted.

Yet many of the objections, justified at the time, may not be valid today, since curriculum change has increased very rapidly during the last decade and basic examining techniques are being improved. The instruments of evaluation are being developed in such a way that the concept of what constitutes 'an examination' is altering. It seems important that methods of evaluation, including awards and examinations, are kept under constant review, and that physical educationists should reconsider their attitude towards them. What was right yesterday may not be right today, and furthermore, what is right in one situation may not be right in another. This article will outline movement studies and consider the problem of examinations in the area, enabling teachers to make their own assessments as to the appropriateness of formal examinations as a means of evaluation.

Movement studies

Human movement is a new field of study; though developed and fostered by physical educationists, it extends beyond their applied study to include such areas as communication through movement, acquisition of skill, personality and movement behaviour, biomechanical analysis, physical work metabolism, play and movement, and work movement. It draws on the physical sciences, the human sciences, philosophy and language forms. Curl (1973) has defined movement study as 'a field of knowledge in which various forms of knowledge converge and cohere in an organic fashion in a mode analogous to the organism itself'. The relationship between physical education, the applied study, and movement studies has been clarified by Arnold (1973), who has delineated three perspectives of movement: perspective I concerned with education through movement; perspective II concerned with education about movement; perspective III concerned with education in movement.

Perspective I he believes to be 'most properly called physical education', that is, the general learning that occurs through taking part in physical activity. By engaging in the traditional activities of gymnastics, athletics, games, dancing, swimming, outdoor activities and other sports, a child will be helped in his socialisation, gain knowledge of self and 'personalise' his knowledge gained through other studies.

Perspective II Arnold describes as the academic study of movement concerned with such matters as how the body moves, how skills are learned and the significance of movement in our daily lives.

Perspective III In this perspective the child will learn and experience skill through movement. Arnold also includes here the development of kinesthetic perception akin to what Morgan *et al.* (1970) term movement sense. Unlike perspective II, this perspective cannot be verbalised. The only way to develop skill, and to experience and become kinesthetically aware is to move oneself. Whereas this awareness is 'inner' and private, physical skill is externally visible and perhaps measurable.

External examinations

Examinations were introduced in the nineteenth century to replace patronage, thus enabling young men to enter the civil service through aptitude. They therefore became instruments of social engineering. In addition, they were seen as a means of raising standards in the schools. Interestingly, in an effort to ensure that swimming and life-saving were taught, the Scholar's Certificate was introduced and described in the illustrated handbook of the Royal Life Saving Society published in 1899. Examinations have always had their critics and the long-standing charges that they were an excuse for poor teaching methods, or that they failed to test the qualities that mattered most, are still heard today. Nevertheless, 'external' examinations are growing in number, though altering in character, and movement study, including physical education, is increasingly found in the lists of subjects from which a child can choose to be examined by GCE or CSE boards.

Perhaps the greatest force for the liberalisation of examinations was the introduction of the Certificate of Secondary Education in 1965. It differs from the General Certificate of Education in that it is administered regionally through fourteen boards (see appendix for names and addresses of these boards) and that it is controlled by practising teachers. In addition, it caters for a wider ability range. It operates in three modes described in a Schools Council publication (Schools Council, 1973):

Mode I examinations conducted by the examining board on syllabuses set and published by the board.

Mode II examinations conducted by the examining board on syllabuses devised by individual schools, or group of schools, but moderated by the board.

Mode III examinations set and marked internally by the individual school, or group of schools, but moderated by the board.

It may not be generally known that GCE boards also operate in modes. For example the Associated Examining Board describe modes similar to the CSE in their regulations. Clearly, then, the stricture that syllabuses and methods of assessment are necessarily laid down by a remote central body is no longer applicable to GCE and CSE examinations, though it is still true of many of the GBA awards.

In external examinations the methods of evaluation, once only the written essay, now include objective tests, practical work, course work, special studies and projects, vivas and group work. Indeed it is possible to take an 'examination' entirely through continuous assessment without a final paper at all. In considering whether to include movement study it is therefore important not to equate an examination solely with the traditional pattern of a terminal written paper, often in the form of essay questions, and calling heavily on the ability to recall factual information.

Examinations in human movement studies

Of the 228 GCE subjects listed as available at 'O' or 'A' level, ballet is the only one that could be considered as coming within the human movement field of study. The CSE mode I list has fewer subjects and the Southern Regional Examinations board is offering physical education as a mode I for the first time in 1977. In addition, schools are increasingly devising a wide variety of syllabuses to be offered under mode III which would come under the umbrella term of movement study, and also some which extend beyond the strict definition of the area to include such topics as 'Sport in Society' which might necessitate, for example, a study of the provision of sports facilities in the community.

Teachers who wish to make a decision as to whether it is feasible and desirable to enter pupils for examinations or awards should first carry out the following procedures:

1 clarify the objectives or expected outcomes of the course,
2 consider possible forms of assessment in relation to the course objectives,
3 weigh up the advantages and disadvantages, taking into account such matters as staffing, time-tabling, facilities, status, and the possible effects on the more able or the less able child.

Objectives of human movement studies

Unless objectives are first established there is a great danger that syllabuses will be moulded to fit the examination procedures, thus warping the course. It is essential that examinations of any kind are servants not masters. Objectives can be considered relative to Arnold's three perspectives: 'through', 'about' and 'in' movement. The first perspective, education through movement, is the most difficult in which to identify objectives, yet some would argue that it is the most central and important of the three. In general we might say that the physical activities engaged in at school can lead to the better social adjustment of the child and what has been described as a condition of 'general educatedness'. Pearce (1972) has pointed out the difficulties of examining such an aspect: 'examinations have to be in subjects and elements of subjects if that is how the school transmits knowledge: there is no practicable way of evaluating any general condition of "educatedness", even if such a condition could be defined.'

Those who believe that perspective I is the most crucial element may dismiss examinations, since they cannot evaluate the most valuable outcome of the movement study curriculum. On the other hand, it can be argued that there is an hierarchical order and that perspective III, education in movement, is a prerequisite to education through movement. If we can provide evidence that a child is educated in movement, we can at least say that the experience may have contributed to a wider personal awareness and understanding of such concepts as 'team spirit' or the nature of games. Perspective II extends beyond the concept of physical education, the applied study, to the wider issues of human movement study. Being interdisciplinary, it draws upon such studies as anatomy, physiology and psychology, traditionally considered examinable,

The task of establishing behavioural objectives in perspectives II and III is very much easier than in perspective I. The following list may be helpful:

1 to perform skilfully,
2 to apply and use skills appropriately,
3 to attain physical fitness,
4 to recall and use propositional knowledge,
5 to observe accurately,
6 to report accurately,

7 to make critical judgments,
8 to arrive at principles and rules from observation and experiment,
9 to foster imaginative and creative abilities.

In order to estimate the balance of a course prior to constructing the instruments of evaluation, it may be helpful to plot objectives against the perspectives as has been done in Table 15.1.

Table 15.1 To show the behavioural objectives of the perspectives

Objectives	Perspectives I	II	III
1 To perform skilfully			X
2 To apply and use skill appropriately			X
3 To attain physical fitness			X
4 To recall and use propositional knowledge		X	
5 To observe accurately		X	
6 To report accurately		X	
7 To make critical judgments		X	X
8 To arrive at principles and rules from observation and experiment		X	X
9 To foster imaginative and creative abilities		X	X

The fact that it is only possible to identify behaviourable objectives in perspectives II and III should in no way undermine the importance of perspective I. However, there is always the danger that formal examinations, by their focus on the development of certain skills and acquisition of knowledge, will cause teachers to lose sight of the more general aims concerned with 'educatedness' of children, perhaps to the distortion of the syllabus.

Methods of evaluation in human movement studies

Having established objectives, it next becomes necessary to consider possible forms of evaluation. These must be considered not only relative to objectives, but also in relation to the stated function of the examination. Tests used to discriminate and act as selective devices may differ from those which are intended to ensure that minimum standards have been achieved. A test only to ascertain the ability to swim a certain distance will differ from one intended to establish how well a child can swim in order to establish an order of merit. In the latter case perhaps, such factors as speed or style will need to be taken into account as well as distances that can be accomplished.

The construction of tests and methods of evaluation is becoming a very much more sophisticated task requiring knowledge of procedures and expertise. Any test must fulfil the following conditions: (1) it must test what it purports to test, (2) it must be consistent, that is, if the test were repeated it should give the same results.

To describe tests in detail, or the principles of their construction, is not within the scope of this article, but in general terms possible types of evaluation are indicated relative to the objectives in Table 15.2.

Table 15.2 To show types of evaluation relative to objectives

Objectives	Types of evaluation
1 To perform skilfully	Practicals
2 To apply and use skills appropriately	Practicals
3 To attain physical fitness	Practicals
4 To recall and use propositional knowledge	Written objective tests
5 To observe accurately To report accurately	Practical, oral or written response. Course work
6 To make critical judgments	Practicals, course work, written essay-type papers
7 To arrive at principles and rules from observation and experiment	Essay-type tests. Course work, projects
8 To foster imaginative and creative abilities.	Practicals, course work, essay-type papers

In any examination the balance given to the different methods must reflect the syllabus and the stated purposes of the assessment. Tests may be limited entirely to practical work, as has been the case in some CSE dance examinations, or tests may include a combination of practicals, course work and a final examination paper as in 'O' level ballet, which has a distribution of marks as follows:

part A, written paper	40 marks
part B, written paper	40 marks
part C, project file	20 marks
part D, practical test	50 marks
total	150 marks

This examination tests both the ability to dance, and critical faculties demanding knowledge about dance, dancers and choreographers. The Southern Regional Examinations Board requires a rather different balance: practical 60 per cent, theory 40 per cent.

If syllabuses are devised, for example in dance, sailing or mountain walking, the content may include other areas of study. Sailing may demand a knowledge of tides and winds; walking the ability to map-read and use a compass; dance a knowledge of companies and choreographers. Such integrated studies would seem not only possible but desirable, since there may be no better way of combining physical and intellectual experience.

Even if it is demonstrated that a syllabus can be evaluated by methods which lend themselves to formalisation in an 'external examination', there are other considerations which may weigh for or against the decision to implement them. It is possible that the most suitable test may prove too expensive to operate. For example, it might be thought best to record performance on film or videotape, but in practice this would be too costly. There is then the danger that less effective tools of assessment may be relied upon. The effect on the school programme must also be considered. Fears have been expressed by some who believe that an examination course in human movement studies would lead to a curtailed activity programme in the school, while others maintain that it might be lengthened, since human movement studies with its practical component would run parallel with other CSE options and would be in addition to, rather than as an alternative to the normal programme. It is certainly important to ensure that no child, whether taking the examination or not, is denied physical activity through pressure on facilities or staff caused by the demands of GCE or CSE groups. The belief that an examination necessarily 'kills enjoyment' would seem to be denied by the fact that there is an enormous voluntary demand to take GBA awards. Children seem to enjoy the reassurance they gain from being measured against national standards. The question of subject status is often raised and in general the views expressed suggest that examinations serve to enhance it. If this point is used as a justification for movement study examinations, it must be shown that this enhancement is of value to the child. Otherwise it can be argued that such examinations are designed for the benefit of subject and teacher rather than for the good of the pupil.

Teachers who are looking at their curricula in human movement studies with a view to 'external examinations' will find most opportunity for experiment and development under mode III regulations. Yet they will be unable to find much direct evidence to help and guide them. Clearly what is needed today, as the demand for GBA awards, CSE and GCE grows, is a rigorously monitored research and development project in the area. Published findings could then go at least some way toward enabling teachers to make informed choices.

Bibliography

Arnold, P. J. (1973), 'Education and the Concept of Movement', in *Bulletin of Physical Education*, vol. IX, no. 5, BAALPE.

Curl, G. (1973), 'An Attempt to Justify Human Movement as a Field of Study', in J. B. Brooke and H. T. A. Whiting (eds), *Human Movement: A Field of Study*, Henry Kimpton, London.

Morgan, R. E. *et al.* (1970), 'The Concept of P.E.', in *British Journal of Physical Education,* vol. 1, no. 4, July 1970.

Pearce, J. (1972), *School Examinations*, Collier-Macmillan, London.

Schools Council (1973), *G.C.E. and C.S.E. A Guide to Secondary-school Examinations for Teachers, Pupils and Employers*, Evans/Methuen Educational, London.

Appendix

Examining boards for the General Certificate of Education

Associated Examining Board, Wellington House, Station Road, Aldershot, Hants.

Joint Matriculation Board, Manchester M15 6EU.

Oxford and Cambridge Schools Examination Board, Elsfield Way, Oxford, and 10 Trumpington Street, Cambridge.

Oxford Delegacy of Local Examinations, Ewart Place, Summertown, Oxford.

Southern Universities Joint Board for School Examinations, Cotham Road, Bristol BS6 6DD.

Irene K. Glaister

University of Cambridge Local Examinations Syndicate, Syndicate Buildings, Cambridge.
University Entrance and School Examinations Council, University of London, 66–72 Gower Street, London WC1 6EE.
Welsh Joint Education Committee, 245 Western Avenue, Cardiff CF5 2YX.

Regional Examining Boards for the Certificate of Secondary Education

Associated Lancashire Schools Examining Board, Refuge Assurance Building, 77 Whitworth Street, Manchester M1 6HA.
East Anglian Examinations Board, The Lindens, Lexden Road, Colchester, Essex.
East Midland Regional Examinations Board, Robins Wood House, Robins Wood Road, Aspley, Nottingham NG8 3NH.
Metropolitan Regional Examinations Board, Lyon House, 104 Wandsworth High Street, London SW18.
Middlesex Regional Examining Board, 53–63 Wembley Hill Road, Wembley, Middlesex HA9 8BH.
North Regional Examinations Board, Wheatfield Road, Westerhope, Newcastle upon Tyne NE5 5JX.
North Western Secondary School Examinations Board, Orbit House, Albert Street, Eccles, Manchester M30 0WL.
Southern Regional Examinations Board, 53 London Road, Southampton SO9 4YL.
South-East Regional Examinations Board, Beloe House, 2 & 4 Mount Ephraim Road, Tunbridge Wells, Kent.
South Western Examinations Board, 23–9 Marsh Street, Bristol BS1 4BP.
Welsh Joint Education Committee, 245 Western Avenue, Cardiff CF5 2YX.
West Midlands Examinations Board, Norfolk House, Smallbrook Queensway, Birmingham 5 4NJ.
West Yorkshire and Lindsey Regional Examining Board, Scarsdale House, 136 Derbyshire Lane, Sheffield S8 8SE.
Yorkshire Regional Examinations Board, 31–3 Springfield Avenue, Harrogate, Yorks HG1 2HR.

16

Certificate of secondary education: syllabus construction in dance

Joan W. White

The Certificate of Secondary Education (CSE) is 'an examination designed to reflect and measure the rising standards of secondary education without inhibiting the school curriculum'.[1]

Introduced in 1965 as a result of the Beloe Report, this was not just another examination, but an attempt to infuse new thinking into the whole concept of examinations and how they should be conducted. As a national examination, CSE is recognised by the Department of Education and Science and all certificates are countersigned on behalf of the Secretary of State. The Schools Council acts as a co-ordinating body to ensure that standards are comparable, but the examination is conducted by fifteen regional examining boards. These are completely autonomous bodies constituted in such a way that all organisations interested in education within the region are represented and the examination is effectively under teacher control. Consequently, CSE is 'the servant of the schools, not their master; it sets out to reflect, measure and enhance the standards in the schools and to encourage their freedom to develop their courses of study in the way they think best for their pupils'.[2]

This school-based philosophy is realised first, due to the fact that those entrusted with the final responsibility for the work in school also control the examinations by which its achievement is measured, i.e. the teachers; and second, schools are able to choose from three modes of examination.

1 External examinations on syllabuses prescribed by the Board—Mode I.

2 External examinations on syllabuses drawn up by individual schools or groups of schools and approved by the Board—Mode II.
3 Examinations set and marked internally by individual schools but moderated at each stage by the Board—Mode III.

A national examination none the less needs a common standard if it is to be accepted generally. This standard cannot be precisely defined but the process is aided by reference to the candidate for whom the examination is intended:

Candidates for C.S.E. generally come from a band of pupils extending from those who are of G.C.E. Ordinary Level standard to those who are a little below average in ability. This is estimated to account for some 60% of all secondary pupils in this country.

Examination performances within this broad band are categorised, the results being expressed in grades 1–5, two of which have been defined by the Schools Council as reference points.

Grade 1—is to be awarded to a pupil whose ability is such that he might reasonably have secured a pass in the G.C.E. Ordinary Level Examination had he followed a course of study leading to that examination instead of C.S.E.

Grade 4—is to be awarded to a pupil of average ability who has followed a course of study for the C.S.E. regarded by teachers of the subject as appropriate to his age, ability and aptitude.

The standards of Grades 2 and 3 are derived from these reference grades, candidates falling between Grades 1 and 4 being awarded Grades 2 and 3 in approximately equal numbers. Grade 5 indicates a performance just below that expected from a pupil of average ability. All other performances are ungraded.[3]

The regional boards ensure that the defined standards of the examination are maintained with reasonable consistency, as a result of which employers and other users of the certificate recognise it as a nationally regulated educational assessment.

Any syllabus constructed for CSE dance naturally must conform to these regulations, but it can be seen that syllabuses may be as many and as varied as the secondary schools in which pupils receive their education and consequently any information given here should be regarded merely as a guide. Points made regarding the process of the submission of syllabuses as such are general, and are likely to vary from one retional examining board to the next.

The first schools to submit a syllabus in dance did so in 1966. At this time (May 1966) a document on CSE dance was prepared by the Laban Art of Movement Guild.[4] This document recommends that the subject should be conducted according to Mode II (i.e. internally set, externally marked) or Mode III (i.e. internally set and marked, externally moderated).

The decision to introduce CSE dance has implications for the teacher, the prospective candidate, the department and the school. Discussion needs to take place with the head of department and other staff directly concerned since hall/gymnasium space is usually required for longer periods. The head teacher, too, should be consulted since time-tabling comparable with other examination subjects should ensue; and at an early stage it is wise to ensure that the subject can be accommodated within the school examination programme. General discussion with the head teacher, the head of department and the school examinations officer is also necessary to determine which mode of examination is considered best to suit the needs of the pupils.

The internal discussions are a prelude to a request to the appropriate regional examining board, who may or may not have a subject committee in dance, but none the less will provide all the specific information required to submit a syllabus (i.e. Mode II or Mode III) for the first time.

Requirements vary, but generally the following details are necessary:

1 The syllabus needs to be headed with the name of the school, the mode of examination, the proposed year of examination and the subject title (i.e. the title to be entered on the candidate's certificate).
2 A brief introduction is required so that the aims of the course may be stated.
3 The content of the syllabus needs to be specified. In dance this usually includes details under the following headings:

Body Dynamics Space Relationship Composition Accompaniment Stimuli	Material of dance which is most generally included.
Historical background Dance styles Notation Anatomy and physiology Related arts Etc.	The inclusion of all or some of these is usually dependent on the interest of pupils and teachers.

It is possible to specify details of the course overall, or as it will be introduced year by year, but it is important to remember that it is an examination syllabus and not a scheme of work for teaching.

4 Examination. A decision must be taken as to the best way in which to examine the syllabus. Generally the work can be divided into practical and theoretical aspects.

(a) Practical 1—Usually this takes place on a particular 'examination day' and might involve the candidate in:

(i) A solo. Choreographed entirely by the candidate. (2 minutes.)
(ii) A study. Possibly teacher-directed.
(iii) Group dance. Choreographed by the candidates.
(iv) Improvisation.

The programme should show the candidate using a variety of stimuli and accompaniment.

2—Coursework. This is the assessment of practical coursework and normally should not receive a high proportion of the final marking, since it is not possible for the board to moderate this work.

(b) Theoretical 1—Coursework. This generally consists of any course notes, written work of a creative nature, diaries of theatre visits, etc.

2—Project. This is written and visual material, collected throughout years IV and V and presented in year V prior to the examination. This may be teacher-guided, but should be chosen by the pupil and show evidence of personal research at CSE level.

3—Paper. Some schools in addition like to have a written paper and for some boards this is necessary for the acceptability of the subject for examination. The paper usually follows a pattern, i.e. three sections—

(i) Compulsory short questions requiring one word or short phrase answers.
(ii) Some choice of questions requiring short paragraph answers.
(iii) Wider choice of questions requiring essay answers.

5 Mark weighting. A clear indication of the mark weighting to be attached to each part of the examination is necessary. Two such examples are given below.

E.g. 1	Practical:	60% i.e.	Solo	20%
			Study	15%
			Group	15%
			Improvisation	10%
	Coursework:	20% i.e.	Practical	10%
			Written	10%
	Project:	20%		
	Total	100%		

E.g. 2	Practical:	60% i.e.	Solo	20%
			Study	15%
			Group	15%
			Improvisation	10%
	Coursework:	15% i.e.	Practical	10%
			Written	5%
	Project:	10%		
	Paper:	15%		
	Total	100%		

If a paper is submitted it is necessary to give the exact mark weighting for each question.

All these details go to the appropriate regional examining board who pass them on to their moderator who, in turn, is requested to comment on the syllabus in a report to the subject committee. A meeting takes place to which the school may be invited, or the moderator may be instructed to contact the school direct. Once the syllabus is agreed, by the school and the moderator, it is adopted by the board and then candidates may be submitted for examination. At the examination (mode III) the teacher assesses the candidates, the moderator merely moderates the grading so that it conforms to the overall standard of the board.

From the time the first decision is made to introduce the examination, to the final acceptance of the syllabus, may take up to eighteen months, though work may start with the candidates in the hope of getting the syllabus through, before the final adoption is confirmed.

The desirability or otherwise of dance as an examinable subject is the topic of much discussion, but for the teacher and pupil alike, an examination, with the degree of flexibility permissible certainly in CSE mode III, can be an exciting project on which to embark and need not be a limitation to the pupil, the teacher or the subject.

Notes

1 Middlesex Regional Examining Board (1971), *Constitution and Regulations*.
2 *Ibid.*
3 *Ibid.*
4 Laban Art of Movement Guild (1966), *Certificate of Secondary Education Examinations in Dance*.

Bibliography

Metropolitan Regional Examining Board (1972) Designations: *Spheres of Responsibility and Conditions of Appointment for Servants of the Board.*
Middlesex Regional Examining Board (1971) *Constitution and Regulations*.
Middlesex Regional Examining Board (1971) *Mode II and Mode III Syllabuses and Examinations—Notes of Guidance*.

17

Evaluation and accountability in physical education

L. Almond

At the present time evaluation and accountability are emotive words in education, and it is quite likely that even more attention will need to be paid to the issues surrounding them as the demand for evaluation and accountability increases. Consequently, in this paper I intend to:

1 trace the historical growth of evaluation concepts;
2 highlight some roles for evaluation;
3 propose a way of looking at school-based evaluation;
4 introduce and examine some issues in the call for accountability.

Everyone evaluates and makes judgments based on personal observation: however, it was during the early 1900s that the concept of evaluation in education began to receive formal definition. During the first thirty years of this century evaluation was concerned with testing pupils using measurement procedures in the form of standardised tests. During the late 1930s a new movement emerged which stressed the compatibility between written statements of educational objectives and achievements. Most attention was devoted to the measurement of attainment, and there was little precise scrutiny of the quality of goals being assessed and the actual effects of a programme.

In the 1960s evaluation became the focus for a new concern: the provision of information for decision-makers. This new focus widened the concerns of evaluation, though most of the developments in this new area can be attributed to the legal requirement (in America) to evaluate all educational programmes and projects which are supported by federal and state funds. Also associated with this movement are judgments of merit concerning analysis of resources (packages of curriculum materials), and the cost-analysis of schemes.

One of the main developments during this period was the rise of 'decision-facilitation' types of evaluation based on a systems and management approach. The key feature of this type of evaluation is that determination of merit is left to the decision-makers: decision-facilitation evaluators are less willing to assess the worth of educational phenomena. Recently, a new version of 'evaluation for informing decision-makers' has emerged. In this new tradition there is a stress on case studies, participant observation, accurate portrayal and sensitive interpretation. It is concerned with the real information needs of a variety of audiences, and aspires to illuminate and portray the real situation. Allied with this new version of evaluation is a concern for 'what is happening in classrooms' which has led to considerable growth in interest about classrooms based on anthropological methodologies. In addition, a number of new projects, 'Progress in Learning Science' and the Ford Teaching Project have emphasised 'learning about learning' and 'learning about teaching'. These developments are of particular interest to the teacher because they directly affect his work in the classroom and closely involve him as an active participant in the research.

This sketch of the development of evaluation can be represented in the following way, and the reader is invited to develop these roles by consulting the references at the conclusion of this paper.

The roles of evaluation

1 The assessment of pupil performance
- (a) status determination
  - (i) achievements
  - (ii) understanding of a course of study (CSE/GCE)
- (b) diagnosis

2 The assessment of goal attainment
- (a) intended outcomes (Tyler)
- (b) Scriven has identified two major deficiencies in the above model
  - (i) quality of goals
  - (ii) goal-free evaluation—the actual effects

3 The provision of information for decision-makers
  (a) comparative evaluation
    (i) a project (Harlen)
    (ii) cost-analysis of schemes (Haller)
    (iii) resources (Eraut)
  (b) decision-facilitation
    (i) countenance (Stake)
    (ii) CIPP (Stufflebeam)
    (iii) CSE (Alkin)
    (iv) discrepancy (Provus)
    (v) transactional (Rippey)
  (c) portrayal of a situation
    (i) illuminative (Partlett)
    (ii) responsive (Stake)
    (iii) democratic (Macdonald)

4 The determination of what is happening in classrooms
  (a) learning about learning
    (i) Man: a course of study approach
    (ii) Progress in Learning Science (Harlen)
  (b) learning about teaching
    (i) Ford Teaching Project (Elliott)
  (c) learning about learning environments (Walberg)

These roles of evaluation are essentially concerned with evaluation conducted by outside experts. If evaluation is to have any significance for the teacher there is a need for curriculum developers to address themselves to the problem of enabling teachers to develop confidence and competence in this new role. In order to do this I should like to propose one way of looking at school-based evaluation.

School-based evaluation

Informal
(a) Self-reflection
  (i) within a subject
  (ii) school policy
(b) Teachers as researchers (linked and supported by outside agencies)
  (i) learning about learning
    (a) pupil growth

(b) focus on learning
(see MACOS and Progress in Learning Science)
(ii) learning about teaching (Ford Teaching Project)

Formal
(a) Resources/cost analysis
(b) Outcomes
(i) achievements
(ii) course of study (CSE/GCE)
(c) Diagnosis
(d) Decision-making processes within the school

The main concern in informal school evaluation is to develop a climate for constructive criticism where teachers can be reflective about their teaching and their beliefs; about what they are trying to achieve; in other words they are studying themselves. It requires a commitment to a particular kind of professionalism—research-based teaching. The teacher as a researcher is a new and demanding role, and although the Ford Teaching Project has shown its value and potential, the problems of such an approach must not be underestimated. It is time consuming, intellectually difficult, and requires security in a potentially threatening situation. Because of these problems the school's first priority is to develop a climate where teachers can be self-reflective about their own teaching. Many schools already adopt such procedures, and more sophisticated ways of enabling teachers to involve themselves in this exercise are beginning to emerge (much of this type of work has been done by the Curriculum Research Unit initiated by Dr J. E. Kane at Loughborough College). When schools have developed this climate it is possible that the idea of the 'teacher as researcher' would be more acceptable and feasible. At the present time it is beyond the capacity of most schools.

Formal systems of evaluation already exist in schools, but it is necessary to develop the potential even further by widening the perspectives of teachers about new forms of assessment for CSE, and new ways of recording progress and presenting data in meaningful ways to teachers and parents. This is a challenge that teachers have taken up, and many interesting developments are occurring. The key problem in both informal and formal school evaluation is the need for a support structure which does not exist at the moment.

Though school-based evaluation has a potential, there are likely to be other types of evaluation by outside agencies, e.g. NFER investigations, Schools Council Project evaluators, and evaluators from the Assessment of Performance Unit initiated by the DES.

Accountability

The call for evaluation and its implications for school-based involvement highlight the notion of accountability. However, what does accountability mean? It seems to imply that teachers are directly responsible for the performance of individuals under their care, and it focuses on the provision of information as an important factor in rendering an account. Obviously, people want to know what is going on because their interests are so manifestly involved: however, this does not mean that they have the right to know. It is sensible and often practicable for a body providing a public service, like schools, to give an account of their activities and make them intelligible to the public. To be accountable is to have a separate duty, over and above the duty of providing a service. This duty exists only where the public is in a position of power. Thus, one can speak of a school being accountable to an LEA and responsible to the public, bearing in mind that this responsibility makes it highly desirable that its activities should be intelligible and well justified.

Thus it would seem that accountability has two concerns, professional accountability and community responsibility. In the first category there is a concern for internal audiences, Head/Governors and LEA, and a form of moral accountability to oneself for one's actions. The classroom teacher may need to ask what it is likely to mean for a school to be accountable for its own curriculum. The second category is concerned with external audiences and identification of the real information needs of these audiences. This is a special problem because schools are associated with a variety of groups, each one having different expectations of what the school is trying to do. How do schools fulfil the demands of all these different groups? Thus the call for accountability raises very specific problems which schools will have to face in the future.

Those who are concerned with evaluation and accountability will have to address themselves to the following questions.

For what should the school be responsible?

(i) What is the purpose of the school?
(ii) What purposes can a school serve?

(iii) How do you cater for different groups who have different expectations for the school?

To whom are schools responsible?

(i) What is the purpose of the evaluation?
(ii) Who is the client of the evaluation?
(iii) How is it to be presented?

How do you demonstrate responsibility?

(i) On what dimensions is the school to be evaluated?
(ii) What are the criteria to be employed?
(iii) What is the role of the evaluator?
(iv) What is expected of the teacher in the evaluation process?

Until we make a start by trying to answer these questions, teachers may find the idea of evaluation threatening and overbearing. However, accountability must be shared, and we must mobilise community support for the schools.

The call for evaluation and accountability is still new, and in this paper I have tried to identify some issues and suggest ways in which school-based evaluation offers a potential for improving schools. This is important, because evaluation does offer potential, but teachers need to be at the heart of its development.

References

The reader will find the following references useful for developing points that I have made in this paper.

D. Hamilton, *Curriculum Evaluation*. Open Books, 1976.
D. Tawney (ed.), *Curriculum Evaluation Today: Trends and Implications*, Macmillan Educational, 1976.
L. Stenhouse, *An Introduction to Curriculum Research and Development*, Heinemann, 1975.

18

Dance as an aspect of physical education

O. M. Chapman

It must first be said that dance appears to sit oddly amongst the other activities of the physical education curriculum, and some writers have argued for its exclusion from the activities, claiming that it should be taught independently as an art form. I would take a more moderate view, that I see dance as an important part of physical education for the primary school child, and in the early years of the secondary school, but that I should hope to see it offered as one of a number of options for boys and girls in the later programme, and the responsibility of a dance specialist (whose specialism may or may not have developed from a background of physical education). The removal of dance would be an impoverishment of physical education.

All movement experience is fundamentally important in the life of children, and when we look at the scope of the activities provided they generally include, for young children, opportunities for gaining mastery of the body in a variety of situations, opportunities for meeting physical challenges, and for the development of skill in handling implements. Dance shares the same medium as activities like games, athletics and swimming and requires similar practical mastery of the body, but dance differs from them in that movement is used not to achieve some practical end, but as a vehicle of artistic expression.

R. E. Morgan (1974) suggests that it is athleticism which dance shares with other activities of the physical education curriculum. He says,

> We think of an athlete and a dancer as being different and

> distinct. Yet the movements of a dancer are, in the truest sense, athletic. They are free, skilful total-body movements and just as obviously as those of the competitive athlete are performed for values found in the movements themselves. . . . Among professional performers there is an unmistakable interest in physical stamina and physical power.

If one is considering activities from a bodily fitness standpoint, certainly great demands need to be made of the body for the purposes of dance, and wider demands are made, for not only must the dancer work with power, he must also develop the ability to move with delicacy and ease. He must not only be able to leap forward and upward, but backwards and sideways; he must be able to use either foot for take-off and landing, the left side of his body must be as versatile as his right. He has to train to land safely from heights, to spin and turn, to fall and adjust his weight immediately in order to rise and dive to the ground again. At times the dancer will accelerate into action from rest, and at other times will have to control the speed of his actions to culminate in a delicate balance. Sometimes gymnastic skills like handstands, body rolls or cartwheels are called for, and sometimes he will have to take risks in launching himself into the air for others to receive and support his weight—no sandpit or piles of plastic foam will cushion his return to earth! Add to all this that his steps (unless sound is called for) must be silent, his sweat unnoticeable, his panting controlled, and one begins to understand that dance is not the effete pursuit that some writers would have us believe. It does not matter if the strain of exertion shows on the athlete (indeed, it seems that for the spectator this is all part of the spectacle), but the dancer in his performance must create an illusion of ease. Dance, seriously undertaken, is a strenuous pursuit and incidentally provides splendid opportunities for the promotion of fitness.

Some writers, notably Russell (1969) and Munrow (1972), have argued that dance is too unlike the other activities for it reasonably to have a place in the physical education scheme. But if one is to exclude one member on these grounds, one would expect that there might be some identifying characteristic which those included might share. It is difficult to see what identifies the co-operative effort of rock-climbers with the competitive exertions of a team game, or again with the gymnast or the ice skater. And what is it that locks the symbolic combat forms of judo, with its ancient rituals, into the physical education programme, but locks out the symbolic forms of dance? The content of the programme is so diverse that Kane (1974), making a study of the relevant literature, assembled a list of eighty different activities; on the basis of those most commonly found they were able only to reduce the list to thirty-five. Amongst those thirty-five activities what is the unifying factor? Some are competitive, others co-operative. Some are team games, others are individual pursuits. Some require an open-air environment, some water, others an indoor space. Most use specialised equipment but some do not. Some symbolise the overcoming of the enemy, one aims literally to overcome the opponent. Most are rule governed, some are not. It is no answer at all to say that the activities are those traditionally found in physical education. In the first place dance has traditionally constituted part of physical education, and sometimes for some people it has been all their physical education; in the second place new activities are constantly added; and in the third it is a very static education which does not question tradition.

If there is any common ground I believe that it is found in that athletic use of the body which I have described, and dance belongs as much to this 'set' as does archery or hockey or swimming. In all the spheres of physical activity the individual uses athletic movement for what is, to him, an intrinsically worthwhile purpose.

Having said all that, it is important that we recognise that it is as a contribution to the aesthetic and creative aspects of education that dance, like all other art forms, has its place. The view, which has gained some currency recently, that the rationale for physical education in the curriculum is as part of aesthetic education is misleading in that, if taken seriously in our teaching it would tend to distort the teaching of activities such as games (where any aesthetic element is incidental to the intrinsic aim of winning) and misleading also in our understanding of what dance is about. To see all physical education activities as aesthetic activities is to miss exactly that which differentiates dance from them as lying within the sphere of the arts, and as being required to be taught and evaluated as an art form. Dance is allied with the other activities within the physical education curriculum, but it is allied with artistic activities without the physical education curriculum, because its primary concern is with aesthetic experience and meaning.

To exclude dance from the programme would be to deprive

physical education of an important and enriching dimension. Children should be given the opportunity within the programme to gain width of experience of using movement, and this should not exclude one way, the artist's way. Munrow (1972) has written,

> Obviously sportsmen and dancers are not identical in their qualities, which does not mean that no sportsman will make a good dancer. But one cannot reasonably doubt that, in terms of self confidence and identification with material, most teachers primarily attracted to one area will do less than justice to the other.

Munrow was writing of the PE student in training, but the argument does, of course, reach further back into the schools for, if we offer a student a one-sided programme in the belief that this is all for which he is fitted, how can he do other than offer a one-sided programme in the schools? I would prefer to see the student, and through him the pupil, given the opportunity to take part both in sporting and artistic activities within the programme and thus able to make his own choice. It might well be that, even at the late age of eighteen, the sportsmen and sportswomen find enjoyment and proficiency in dance in addition to their sport, and do not wish to make a choice between them. It has been found over a number of years of teaching physical education students within a physical education department that dance, for them, is as purposeful and satisfactory a pursuit as the other areas of the curriculum and as teachable to subject; the problem for them is often choice of specialisation in the third year. (I am aware that in this country traditionally there are cultural differences for men, but the evidence begins to point towards an increasing and less inhibited interest on the part of young men, and if they are helped to feel secure in the dance situation they are no more and no less self-conscious in the initial stages than young women who are also making a beginning in dance.) It is a strange and, I had thought, outmoded view of education, to hold that the person who is accomplished in one pursuit is unlikely to have enthusiasm for or success in another. My impression is that current educational practice favours the integration of subjects rather than their isolation from each other, and what could be more integrated than a physical education programme which offers a field of study based on man's enjoyment of action?

The teacher's view of the intrinsic nature of dance is likely to affect the content and methods he uses, and it is therefore important, I believe, for the teacher to understand that he is dealing with an art form as he would if he were teaching music or ceramics or painting. We have moved a long way in our thinking since the *Syllabus of Physical Training for Schools* (1919) said, 'Dancing if properly taught, is one of the most useful means of promoting a graceful carriage with free, easy movements.' The *Syllabus* for 1934 developed the same theme:

> As well as being stimulating, dancing requires a nicety in adjustment of effort and smooth sequence and blending of movement, which cannot fail to increase the power of coordination. . . . Dancing well taught should result in the loss of self-consciousness and thus help the student to manage herself to better advantage in the ordinary movements of daily life.

And yet the utilitarian view of dance as a kind of fitting of the body for its better use in everyday life or in other activities still has a counterpart today in Keep Fit exercises to music and games training to music. The Keep Fit movement provides enjoyable exercise for thousands of women, and claims for the efficacy for boys and men of musical games training may be found to be true; but we should be aware that, whilst exercises to music may sometimes be an appropriate method for the practice of technique, unless they lead to dance seriously offered as an art they are unconnected with the educational purpose of initiation into the art of dance.

David Best (1974) makes this point differently when he says,

> When we are considering a work of art from the aesthetic viewpoint we are not considering it in relation to some external function or purpose it serves. The work of art cannot be evaluated aesthetically according to its degree of success in achieving some such extrinsic end.

Boys and girls are outside the sphere of artistic education when the primary aim is the achievement of bodily fitness or the pleasurable acquisition of games skills. Teachers are mistaken not when they include dance in physical education, but when they misunderstand its role, and I believe that it is such a misunderstanding which has sometimes been responsible for the failure of dance to 'catch on'. The teacher requires understanding of dance as an art form, and to see his purpose as initiating children into that art form. The teacher needs knowledge, depth of knowledge, so that he may on the one hand introduce children to a gradually increasing mastery of movement, and on the other that he may help children to gain an increasing ability to make choices and to organise material into a coherent whole. Additionally, as H. B. Redfern (1973) has commented, children require help in 'imaginative looking and listening'. The writer notes the neglect of this facet of dance education in our schools today and says,

> There is too perhaps a failure to recognize that a child's concept of what a dance *is* is likely to be unduly impoverished if there are few opportunities to see and appraise the more accomplished work of others. One has only to consider how poverty stricken our notions of music and poetry would be if these had been limited to what we ourselves had invented; and to recall the marked improvement and desire to improve that often attend children's own efforts following the extension of their experience in this way. Conversely, creating and performing dances would seem likely to contribute to imaginative looking. Thus the practical and appreciation aspects are mutually enriching.

There should be three strands, then, in the knowledgeable teaching of dance: opportunity for children to gain skill in the dancer's craft, opportunity to make choices and critical judgments, and opportunity to apply judgment, not only to one's own works, but to the works of accomplished artists.

In the primary school I would not hope or expect to find a specialist dance teacher, but would hope that the class teacher would include dance in the physical education programme regularly. The good primary school teacher generally encompasses all areas of knowledge with his class and, although some degree of specialisation is often found (particularly in the later age groups and in middle schools) usually classes do not go without art or literature or history because the teacher is not a specialist in these areas, and it is to be hoped that this would be true of dance. In the team teaching situation excellent opportunities are created whereby teachers may contribute their expertise, and learn from the contribution of others. At this stage of the children's learning there will be most emphasis on the practical imaginative doing of dance. But the imaginative looking side could be furthered particularly by bringing into the school some of the touring companies which specialise in this kind of work, and by follow-up in later lessons.

A factor which I believe has mitigated against the development of structured dance teaching in the primary school is the misuse of the radio lessons 'Movement and Music' and 'Movement, Mime and Music'. Doubtless these broadcasts provide useful material both in the provision of ideas and the use of musical extracts (and BBC figures prove their popularity), but unless the teacher uses them critically and carefully they have little to do with the art of dance. This is not the fault of the programme planners, but of the physical circumstances of broadcast lessons. An essential element in dance teaching is clearly that of observation, and this, of course, is the very element that can never be present in a broadcast lesson. The teacher requires skill in observation of what the children actually do, so that he may help them in experimenting and practising and give further suggestions at the appropriate time, and the children require time and practice in observation if they are to learn to make choices and critical judgments. Both children and teachers need time and opportunity to observe and discuss and consolidate what is created. None of these requirements, which are clearly fundamental, can be satisfied by broadcast lessons, unless the teacher spends considerable time making selections from the taped broadcast, and uses them with discrimination supplemented strongly by his own teaching. There has been a great deal of excellent work done in the field of dance in our primary schools, but the increasing skill and understanding which results stems from the participation of both children and teacher in a joint artistic experience.

At the secondary school stage the teacher requires more knowledge and expertise, and dance teaching must become the work of someone who has received considerable dance education in his own physical education course. For many years dance education has had a major share in women's courses and happily there are now many colleges of education in which men and women students take part together in main courses of physical education, and there is therefore some hope that boys as well as girls may at least participate sufficiently in dance for them to choose freely whether or not they wish to pursue it, either in a practical way in school or as members of an informed audience.

At this point I wish to say something about what kind of dance should be taught. I think it is the task of the school to provide boys and girls with a broad view of dance, again so that they may learn to discriminate and select for themselves, both as practitioners and as audience. There has been some pressure in recent years for one style of dance to take precedence in schools; the pressure has been resisted, and I believe rightly so. The reasons for this resistance are several. The first is that a dance style, whether the style of Scottish dancing, or the Martha Graham style, or the classical ballet style, or even the style of modern 'pop' dancing, always constitutes a selection from the multitude of ways in which a human being may move. Although it may be entirely appropriate for a young person who intends to enter a professional company to be trained in that particular selection of ways of moving, it is inappropriate and limiting for the ordinary person. It is as inappropriate as it would be to train the young painter to paint only in the style of Picasso. Second, it is clear that I see dance education as having several aspects: experimenting, creating, performing and appreciating, all have a part to play. But when the emphasis is on training a style, performing takes precedence, creating in the medium comes last. When one sees today the glorious work in painting and modelling displayed in our schools, reads the poetry and prose, hears the music being made, it would seem unfortunate if only the art of dance were confined to an interpretative role and pupils were never given the scope to use the language of dance for the articulation of their own ideas. It is not by such limited means that new choreographers or open-minded audiences are made. Third, it is likely that the majority of the young people who find enjoyment in dance in school, if their interest continues, will later become not dancers, not choreographers, but audiences for the dance. How much more informed an audience will they be if they are able to look at dance, not through the narrow window of one dance style, but through a broad view of what constitutes dance in general.

What is needed is a scheme of dance education which focuses on the material of movement itself and gives some order to general categories of movement which seem to be fundamental in the language of dance. Consideration must be given in any way of dancing to the way in which the parts of the body act both in relation to themselves and to the floor and the space surrounding the body; the dynamics of rhythm and phrasing is another important category; and the direction and pattern of movements can be analysed in any style of dance. When Rudolf Laban (1948) recommended that 'instead of studying each particular movement, the principle of moving must be understood and practised', this was the kind of approach that he intended. He was not advocating a new style of dance to replace other established dance styles which are suited to the professional theatre, he was advocating a new approach to the art of dance in general. Those of us who have based our teaching on his theories do not see ourselves as teaching 'the Laban method', but as using those theories because they are the ones which most meet the educational need for a broad perspective on the art of dance. Laban's theories are not regarded as definitive edicts, but as useful working material which is constantly being questioned. It is useful to turn again to H. B. Redfern (1973) who says

> Laban's proposals . . . should not, however, be regarded as the blueprint for all time—nor indeed, judging by Laban's own remarks, were they intended as such. But they might be taken to illustrate the *kind* of scheme required. There is no reason why they have to be adopted just as they stand (many practitioners, while retaining his general classification, already reject the thematic approach), nor why Laban's plan should not be modified in other ways, and developed and used in conjunction with other systems which seek to further understanding of the elements of movement relevant to dance, and to stimulate new ways of composing and looking at dance.

Dance, taught from such an educational stance, seems to me to have an important place in the physical education programme. Where many of our women physical education teachers (and increasingly some men) have acquired artistry and expertise it is my hope that they will be given not less, but increasing opportunities to introduce this rich and imaginative dimension of physical education to their pupils.

Bibliography

Best, David (1974), 'The Aesthetic in Sport', *British Journal of Aesthetics*, Summer 1974.

Board of Education (1919), *Syllabus of Physical Training for Schools*.

Board of Education (1934), *Syllabus of Physical Training for Schools*.

Kane, J. (1974), *Physical Education in the Secondary School* (Schools Council Research Studies), Macmillan.

Laban, R. (1948), *Modern Educational Dance*, Macdonald & Evans.

Morgan, R. E. (1974), *Concerns and Values in Physical Education*,

G. Bell.
Munrow, A. D. (1972), *Physical Education*, G. Bell.
Redfern, H. B. (1973), *Concepts in Modern Education Dance*, Henry Kimpton.
Russell, J. (1969), *Creative Dance in the Secondary School*, Macdonald & Evans.

19

Accompaniment for dance

H. W. Wilkinson

Considerable confusion can arise between the terms accompaniment and stimulus. The aim of this article is to deal with different aspects of accompaniment for dance and will not approach the question of suitable stimuli. The role of accompaniment is to heighten, underline and help to establish mood and meaning. But the dance does not arise from such accompaniment and may even have been choreographed before the accompaniment has been considered.

It is very important in the educational field that children should be exposed to, and employ, as wide a range of accompaniment as possible. If they are helped to use such accompaniment sensitively their general awareness of dynamics and form is developed and their appreciation and understanding of movement increased; they are encouraged to exercise a whole range of sensory apparatus.

From earliest times dance has often been accompanied by some kind of sound. Music is said to have arisen from dance, from the inherent rhythmic urge in man which naturally found its expression in dance and the vocal and bodily sounds which resulted from such movement. But it must be recognised that dance can exist in its own right without sound of any kind. Marion North (1973) suggests: 'Not only is sound accompaniment not always necessary, but very often the intrusion of sound, particularly if it is less refined than the movement patterns, will limit the movement rather than enhance it.'

The voice is one of the most flexible forms of accompaniment. Teachers are aware of how much the pitch and quality of their voice can affect children's responses. The ability to match the quality of vocal sound to the movement response required is an essential element of successful dance teaching. The human voice is the most personal and immediate means of sound making, being capable of infinite variations and stresses. Accommodation can be made straight away by the teacher to the varying reactions of the class, and emphasis can be given where it is needed together with the use of illustrative words which could reinforce the initial stimulus.

Children naturally accompany their own movements with body percussion and voice sounds. The authors of the publication *Movement* (DES, 1972) write of the duality of dance and body sounds in this way:

> The unity of sound and movement is demonstrated by the sounds which arise from the body itself—from the breath and vocal organs in hard rhythmic effort, from the feet moving over the surface of the ground, and from parts of the body as they strike or glance past each other (p. 56).

Much can be developed from clapping rhythms using different areas of the body, and incorporating such actions as stamping, brushing and clicking. The production of his own vocal accompaniment will often increase the involvement of the child in his chosen activity. Young children can be introduced gradually to various rhythms which develop the notions of phrasing and sequence making. Suggestions as to how they begin, what happens, how they come to an end, serve as stable ideas of construction.

Vocal and bodily accompaniment are sometimes used in connection with other ideas such as fireworks, where the addition of sound helps the quality of the movement response. There is a definite stage in children's development when sound and action are closely related. This form of accompaniment is particularly suited to young children as it allows a completely unhindered approach to the dance experience in which they are involved, with no necessity to conform to any kind of external class rhythm. The children are left completely free to work in their own personal rhythms. The older children in the secondary school find that the use of the voice in relation to certain dance sequences they have created aids clarification and results in heightened participation.

Percussion instruments provide a very straightforward, easily comprehended form of accompaniment. The use of single instruments can support many experiences in the area of quality of movement, underlining the forcefulness or delicacy, suddenness or sustainment, directness or flexibility, constraint or otherwise of the movement. Children can become accustomed to the establishment of a phrase and to repetition, and gradually the ability to memorise movement develops. If the teacher is playing the instrument he must be aware of how to initiate, develop and bring the phrase to an end, and be able to repeat it accurately. The importance of the placing of a climax within the phrase must be clearly recognised. Whenever percussive accompaniment is used the teacher needs to ensure that his own movement involvement, although minor, is obvious, so helping both the children's response and his own playing. Care must be taken to employ a variety of rhythms, particularly those which are not characteristic of the teacher, so that the children are exposed to a wide range of dynamic structures.

Whenever possible enough percussion should be available for each child to have an instrument. Much can be done in the classroom to improvise equipment using such things as containers filled with different materials, pieces of wood, tin plates or loops of curtain rings. The making and decorating of the instruments provide an opportunity for the involvement of other areas of the curriculum. The individual use of percussion gives a unique opportunity to every child to create his own accompaniment, and through this activity to become more aware of the qualities inherent within the movement phrase he has formed.

On some occasions children can accompany each other once the individual movement phrase has been established. This activity is of great value, as in so doing the player is put in the position of having to observe and be sensitive to the nuances of the dancer's idea, and of attempting to translate the movement pattern into matching or complementing sound.

The nature of various rhythms must be understood so that the teacher can make a suitable choice for the task in hand. Two beats in a bar basically encourages an accompaniment of a somewhat square, ongoing nature, the emphasis often being on one side of the body. Whereas a grouping of three beats tends to promote a more flowing type of response, causing the emphasis to change from one side of the body to the other. The grouping of five or seven beats where there is a mixture of duple and triple — — / — — — or — — — / — — — — can help the development of irregular, asymmetric movement together with a pronounced feeling of change and excitement. It is necessary to take cognisance of these basic factors when selecting a suitable accompaniment for a particular dance.

The placement of accents within a phrase can make or mar the class's achievement of the task set. Any form of elevation, for example, can be helped by a syncopated use of accents, the stronger beat being placed on the second half of the first beat of the bar, the first marking the take-off, the second the height of the jump. Lack of a clear accent tends to produce monotony, vagueness of form and an inconclusive ending.

Care must be taken to provide both metrical forms of accompaniment and those which have a freer rhythmic structure. Some children find accommodation to a metrical beat difficult but can respond easily to a less arbitrary division of time. This is particularly true of the younger children in our schools.

As children become able to work satisfactorily in groups a more elaborate use of percussion can be employed. A group composition can be enhanced by the working out of quite complex accompaniment, which could either be taped or played by a separate group. This can be composed either parallel to the choreographing of the dance or afterwards when the composition is established. Top juniors and secondary school children can gain a great deal from this experience in awareness both of what the dancers are trying to communicate and of how to use sound to underline meaning. They begin to realise the need to consolidate the rhythmical aspects, to select appropriate tempi and to be sensitive to the quality of sound needed. Group percussion can also provide an accompaniment which deepens the mood the dancers wish to create without approximating too rigidly to the actual motifs of the dance.

The transient nature of music and dance has resulted in a close relationship being established between these two art forms. Music is often the first form of accompaniment to be considered, because of its traditional involvement with dance both in the social sphere and in the theatre. Obviously the choice of music is governed partly by the age of the children, and by their interests and experience. Music for young children should be simple, clear and short. Very often children in the first school are not ready to make positive use of any musical accompaniment provided. Brearley *et al.* (1969) remind us that music should be used sparingly with young children, as this is the time in their development when they are occupied in establishing their own personal rhythms and find it difficult to conform to a highly structured sound of someone else's making. Few children are at the stage when they are aware of phrasing except in the most obvious way, but a simple rhythm can be meaningful. Music of a clear and very definite character is desirable, and there should be, wherever possible, ample repetition. Complex orchestration tends to prove too difficult for children in the first school, as it provides too diffuse, and sometimes too involved a form at a time when they are often dealing with one criterion at a time. Attention needs to be paid to melody; children show considerable appreciation of a simple melodic line such as they learn in nursery rhymes, and enjoy the opportunity for repetition and reiteration. There are a number of record series which have been found by practising teachers to provide very suitable accompaniment for a wide range of dance ideas.

As children reach the middle years of schooling it is important that a considerable variety of musical accompaniment is employed. The music should be short and clear in mood and rhythm but have scope for development. Children in secondary school are capable of appreciating the full range of music available, and their ability to respond to difficult contemporary forms should not be underestimated. Electronic music provides a good example: many children find such music a very satisfactory choice of accompaniment and it seems to give the right kind of support for many ideas about which they want to dance, as, of course, does some 'pop' music.

Choosing music for dance is an extremely time-consuming process. Great care has to be exercised to find exactly the right piece for the proposed study or dance. There are many aspects which need to be considered, for example the kind of dance which is to be undertaken and whether it is dramatic, abstract or lyrical. Music suitable for a dance drama will probably have a considerable stress on mood, the dynamic and textural content being of prime importance, whereas music for a lyrical dance or for spatially structured studies might have a more melodic stress. The form of the dance must also be considered. Two related ideas often demand music in a binary form; the rondo allows for either a constant return to the original idea or it can provide opportunities for the establishment of a 'chorus'. Music composed in the form of theme and variations is often extremely useful for a dance study where a restricted area of movement needs to be examined and worked out in several different ways.

The rhythmical character of a piece of music is also important. As mentioned previously in the discussion on percussion, duple time can promote movement of an even, martial nature whereas triple time can enhance and encourage more flowing, travelling lyrical movement. Irregular rhythms provide an accompaniment of a more restless, exciting kind, combining as they do elements of both duple and triple time. A decision regarding the tempo required is also necessary, as there is a marked difference in mood between music played at a fast tempo and that performed in a more deliberate manner.

It is important that once an accompaniment has been introduced the teacher should not encourage a too close relationship with the actual structure of the piece. The dance should not be just a replica or interpretation of the music but should be developed independently, whilst still maintaining a relationship with both the form and the mood of the music used. The accompaniment must always support and help but not dominate, leaving the dancer room to create and develop his own ideas. The role of accompaniment in the dance lesson is perhaps a little different from its position in a dance performance. In relation to dance performance M. D'Houbler (1962) suggests that: 'as an accompaniment the music is the means of helping the observer to sense the dancer's thought and feeling—one more sense perception added to the visual and the kinaesthetic' (p. 158).

There is no reason why, with the co-operation of a sympathetic school music department, the children should not compose accompaniments for their own dances, so giving a further dimension to their creative work in music. The composition of musical accompaniment can contribute much to children's awareness of, and sensitivity to, all forms of sound, heightening their response to such things as tone, pitch, harmony, form and rhythm.

Although the services of an accompanist are often extremely valuable, care must be taken to enable him to understand and be sensitive to the movement ideas that are to be explored. Any pianist or percussionist who is able to improvise for movement is a very great asset, as the teacher is able to draw upon flexible and spontaneous support for any ideas she or the class wish to pursue.

Other forms of accompaniment such as voice sounds, choral speaking and singing can be used. Lighting can provide an exciting addition to dance, promoting mood, highlighting climaxes and providing transitions. Projected slides can supplement mood and meaning very effectively. Interesting experiments are now taking place in the contemporary theatre which could suggest many new ideas to the enterprising teacher of dance. A decision must also be made as to whether any accompaniment at all is necessary, or if the class needs to be allowed complete freedom to establish the form, length and rhythmic structure of their dances. V. Bruce (1970) suggests that 'sometimes children must be free to move and dance unhampered by music or any other external sound accompaniment'.

In an article of this length there is not time to do more than indicate some of the various approaches to accompaniment that are possible. Much care needs to be taken when selecting the form that the accompaniment should take, as it is such a very important element in the success or failure of a dance lesson, having the power to enhance or adversely affect the response of the children. Very little research has been carried out into the relationship between dance and accompaniment. Perhaps some research needs to be carried out in an area which has the potential to contribute so much to the development of children's perceptual awareness.

Bibliography

Beat, J. (1970), 'An extension of vocal accompaniment to dance', *Laban Art of Movement Guild Magazine*.

Brearley, M. *et al*. (1969), *Fundamental in the First School,* Blackwell.

Brocklehurst, B. (1971), *Response to Music*, Routledge & Kegan Paul.

Bruce, V. (1970), *Movement in Silence and Sound*, G. Bell.

DES (1972), *Movement*, HMSO.

D'Houbler, M. (1962), *Dance, A Creative Art Experience*, University of Wisconsin Press.

Goodridge, J. and Cox, B. (1973), 'Notes on some aspects of movement and sound', *Laban Art of Movement Guild Magazine*.

Horst, L. (1968), 'Pre-Classic Dance Forms', *Dance Horizons*.

Horst, L. and Russell, F. (1961), 'Modern Dance Forms', *Dance Horizons*.

Leonard, M. (1971), 'Rhythm and Dance', *Laban Art of Movement Guild Magazine*.

Morley, J. (1972), 'Music, dance and speech—a Unity', *Laban Art of Movement Guild Magazine*.

North, M. (1973), *Movement Education*, Macdonald & Evans.

Turner, M. (1971), *New Dance*, University of Pittsburgh Press.

20

Physical education, human movement and integrated studies

Alan Gibbon

The topic the editor has presented me with bristles with problems of all kinds, not least semantic ones. In a handbook of 'movement studies' I have been asked to write about 'physical education', 'human movement' and 'integrated studies'. I will begin by exploring the relationship between the burgeoning area of 'human movement' or 'movement studies', which I will presume are one and the same thing, and the subject, still usually called 'physical education', that is part of the curriculum of all primary and secondary schools in this country.

It shouldn't be necessary to explain to readers of this handbook that under the title 'physical education' I embrace the activities called 'games', that still appears alongside 'PE' on school timetables. I also include 'dance' for the purposes of this paper, though in many schools it has become established as a subject and department in its own right. I do not include 'movement' because as an activity taught to children, I have never discovered what it is. It is sad that physical educationists have, in a fairly short period of time, managed to come up with such a variety of terms to describe what it is they do (I haven't mentioned 'basic movement', 'modern educational dance' and 'inventive movement') and not surprising, therefore, that 'PT', rejected by the profession over a quarter of a century ago, is still commonly used by the general public and the media.

For a survey of the 'state of play' in the 'physical education—human movement' debate the reader should look at two fairly short papers; first Gordon Curl's chapter in a book *Human Movement: A Field of Study*[1] and, second, Peter

Renshaw's chapter in a very recently published book *Curriculum Development in Physical Education.*[2] Curl, accepting Hirst's categorisation of knowledge into seven distinct forms, presents a case for human movement as a field of knowledge—that is, a secondary construct of the basic forms: for Curl, physical education is an application of human movement in an educational context. The attraction of this account is clear to those in institutes of higher education who would like to pursue their 'pure' research into human movement unhindered by the problems and distractions of relating it to the kinds of physical activities engaged in by children at school and by children and adults in their leisure time. The research can then be written up and published in their own *Journal of Human Movement*: 'Right arm superiority for tapping with distal and proximal joints'[3] is the kind of useful research that appears in this journal.

Renshaw doubts whether the various forms of knowledge that might contribute to an understanding of human movement 'converge and cohere in an organic fashion, in a mode analogous to the organism itself'.[4] I think that means that Renshaw doesn't think that Curl's case is a good one. Renshaw appears to accept totally the evaluative function of education, in which it is pursued to 'develop certain intrinsically desirable qualities of mind based on a breadth of knowledge and understanding'.[5] On this score, aims of physical education such as the promotion of fitness and health, the acquisition of neuromuscular skill and the formation of a positive attitude towards physical activity cannot 'masquerade as valid aims of physical education'.[6] Of course they can't if one first accepts, as complete and all-embracing, the evaluative concept of education which stresses, above all, the development of mind and ignores or, at best, devalues other aspects of what it is to be human.

Peter Arnold has challenged what he calls the 'Initiation Model of Education'[7] as not so much wrong as inadequate. He believes that it is deficient on two major counts: first, that 'it makes the mistake of tending to ignore the concept of a person with an intellectualistic account of mind', and second that 'it emphasises mind at the expense of body which . . . is an integral part of what it is to be human'.[8] Of course the systematic development of physical skills in children through programmes of physical education should not be reduced, as it was and so often still is, to mindless physical training or conditioning. It should progress hand in hand with a proper appreciation of, and insight into, the activities in a very wide sense; but appreciation and insight that stems, above all, from 'first hand engagement in them'.[9]

Teachers toiling away in their schools to do just this will, if they have the time, inclination and, not least, mastery of the jargon, to follow the debate, probably be profoundly depressed. What on earth has it all got to do with their work in schools? What is wrong with a belief that physical skill, presented and developed through a rationally conceived, balanced and challenging programme of activities, should be the cornerstone of any argument they may have for a significant place in the 'compulsory' curriculum of schools? Why shouldn't physical skill be recognised as 'a distinct type of awareness that calls upon the kinaesthetic apparatus and which permits the individual to understand and know himself better'[10]—a way of knowing that challenges the domination that intellectual knowledge has over the curricula of our secondary schools; a dominance that goes unchallenged because so many within physical education appear to be more interested in finding a place in the academic sun by establishing 'The Royal Society for the New Science of Movement'[11] than in supporting their colleagues in schools who still believe in a 'field of activity in which physical sensation, fun, beauty and opportunities for training fuse to promote an enrichment of living which encompasses education for the growing child'.[12]

If physical skill is the main aim why should it not be underpinned by a rediscovered and redefined concept of physical fitness? There does appear to be a growing body of empirical evidence of the value of physical fitness in any concept of positive health for urban man in his stressful environment. Not only can it enhance the quality of life; it can contribute to the delay of degenerative heart conditions—'The Western Way of Death'.[13] If these twin aims—physical skill underpinned by physical fitness—are pursued vigorously through carefully structured programmes of physical activity, physical education has a chance of making a unique contribution to the enrichment of life.

I now turn to the question of physical education and integrated studies. 'Integration' is, of course, an approval word among curriculum developers and is particularly favoured for the very young and the not so bright (the 'Newsom' children). It has been far less enthusiastically embraced by those committed to public examinations; even Schools Council projects, supported by generous resources, have found it difficult to introduce and sustain in schools. Marten Shipman's recent book which tries to get 'inside a curriculum project' highlights vividly the problems of achieving any kind of innovation in schools, let alone innovation across traditional boundaries.[14] One suspects that successful innovations involving integration (rather than interdisciplinary enquiry) are very rare indeed anywhere in the curriculum.

Richard Pring's chapter on 'Curriculum integration' in R. S. Peters's book *The Philosophy of Education*[15] hints at the muddle and confusion the whole business of 'integration' raises in educational discussion and clarifies some of the complex issues involved. However, for the purposes of this paper I turn to R. C. Whitfield in his rather patchy book *Discipline of the Curriculum*[16] for a useful distinction between integration and interdisciplinary study. The former, he says,

> implies a merging or thorough inter-mingling of subjects, a '*blending*' or hybridization of things which at present stand apart, whereas the latter implies '*collaboration*' and a viewing of topics from logically different viewpoints. Integrated study requires a synthesis of material; inter-disciplinary study leaves this to occur when meaningfully possible for the individual teacher.

Where then in schools today is physical education involved in integration and where in interdisciplinary study?

Accepting for the purposes of this paper that dance at school level is usually part of physical education, it is clearly in this area that physical education reaches out to the other creative or expressive arts in the sharing or blending of form, techniques and symbols. However, even in this potentially fertile area there is almost certainly need for an adequate experience and understanding of the individual art forms before any truly integrated work can be attempted successfully. Unless 'each art form flourishes in its own right and . . . there is dialogue and co-operation between staff . . . an imposed general mish-mash of well meaning but spineless integration, a mixed media democracy where everything operates at the lowest common denominator'[17] is likely to be the result. This last statement was made by Alec Davison, director of the Cockpit Arts Workshop in London which has become a focus for integration of the arts at all levels. In the article from which the quotation is taken he is introducing to London teachers a publication which is both optimistic and realistic about the problems of integration in the creative arts.

A quotation from it takes one straight back to the implications for schools of the reorganisation and academicisation of initial teacher preparation.

> Anyone in this field [expressive arts] growingly realises the inadequacy of most of the college training and its lack of relevance to the classroom situation. With only a few exceptions in each of the subject areas there seems to be a deficiency of courses which are centrally practical, creative and experimental, which are focused on child development through contact and observation, which tease out of practice the nature of group dynamics and an understanding of play, creativity, language, oracy, moral education and aesthetics and which develop the case of the art form as a tool for other content learning. In fact, there is a national dearth of courses that are creative and educational. Too often they can be a hotch-potch of other intellectual disciplines, academic in flavour and approach, and easily assessable for final examinations.[18]

Interdisciplinary study, as defined by Whitfield, is more common in schools and probably more easy to introduce and sustain than genuine integrated study, though one should not underestimate the problems secondary teachers particularly face in establishing innovation of this kind. Topic-centred studies can be superficial and trivial without some understanding of the various disciplines which will give insight into the nature of the topics. Anyone who has tried to find, let alone introduce and sustain, successful examples of interdisciplinary studies in secondary schools, will not be unduly optimistic about the rapid spread of such an approach to learning in secondary schools.

One example of a reasonably successful interdisciplinary course in physical education was stimulated by the raising of the school leaving age. One of the areas of the course, human performance, consisted of laboratory work, practical sessions, seminars and tutorials and was primarily concerned with the scientific examination and assessment of physical fitness, fatigue, attention and arousal, motor skill and motivation. So that the students would not get bogged down in pure theory, the approach to these factors of human performance was based on the analysis of observable activities such as the performance of a footballer or athlete. A sport and society area concentrated on an investigation of the interaction of sport and society in the modern world, and discussion and seminars covered such topics as the effects of race, politics and nationalism on sport and the roles of amateur and professional sportsmen. Surveys of recreational activities were carried out and extended forward into prediction about future requirements. One LEA is now introducing a CSE course entitled 'Sport and Society' which, like the one described, is largely concerned with interdisciplinary study involving a grasp of different kinds of propositional and practical knowledge, but which is built upon, and springs from, engagement in challenging, progressive, vigorous and stimulating programmes of physical activity.

References

1 Curl, G. F. 'An Attempt to Justify Human Movement as a Field of Study', in Brooke, J. D. and Whiting, J. T. A. (eds), *Human Movement: A Field of Study*, Henry Kimpton, London, 1973.

2 Renshaw, P., 'Human Movement Studies and the Curriculum', in J. Kane (ed.), *Curriculum Development in Physical Education*, Crosby Lockwood Staples, London, 1976.

3 Kimera, D. and Davidson, W., 'Right Arm Superiority for Tapping with Distal and Proximal Joints', *Journal of Human Movement*, vol. 1, no. 4, December 1975.

4 Renshaw, P., *op. cit.*, p. 62.

5 *Ibid.*, p. 63.

6 *Ibid.*, p. 65.

7 Arnold, P., 'Intellectualism, Holism and Movement, or A Critique of the Initiation Model of Education', in the *Bulletin of Physical Education*, vol. XI, no. 1, January 1975.

8 Arnold, P., *op. cit.*, p. 13.

9 *Ibid.*, p. 10.

10 *Ibid.*, p. 15.

11 White, J. P., *Towards a Compulsory Curriculum*, Routledge & Kegan Paul, London, 1973.

12 Morgan, R. E., *Concern and Values in Physical Education*, G. Bell, London, 1975.

13 Carruthers, M., *The Western Way of Death*, Davis-Poynter, London, 1972.

14 Shipman, M. with Bilam, D. and Jenkins, D., *Inside a Curriculum Development Project*, Methuen, London, 1974.

15 Pring, R., 'Curriculum Integration', in Peters, R. S., *The Philosophy of Education*, Oxford University Press, London, 1973.

16 Whitfield, R. (ed.), *Disciplines of the Curriculum*, McGraw-Hill, London, 1971.

17 Davison, A., 'Creativity and Integration', in *ILEA Contact*, vol. 3, issue 8, 28 June 1974.

18 Davison, A., 'Making it Possible', in *The Creative Arts in the Secondary School*, ILEA, 1974.

21

The teaching of adapted physical education

Dudley F. Cooper

At a stage in history when Man's concern for the care of Man is greater than it has ever been it is not surprising that physical education should find new challenges in contributing to the health and happiness of the handicapped. What is surprising, however, is the discovery of how little contribution has been made in the past and the relatively small amount of research into the value of physical activity for such people. There are signs, though, that the situation is changing fairly rapidly, and the Physical Education Association's 1973 New Year Conference on 'Exceptional Children'[1] may well be seen as a landmark in the history of adaptive physical education in this country.

The above comments on the relatively small amount of work and research are, of course, generalised, for in some fields, particularly the physically handicapped, workers appear to have been convinced many years ago of the beneficial value of physical activity. Much of the credit for this must be attributed to a non-physical educationist, Sir Ludwig Guttman, for his inspiration and promotion of sport and recreation in the physical, social and psychological rehabilitation of the physically handicapped. Though dealing mainly with paraplegics he has shown that it is quite feasible for those confined to wheelchairs to take part in such diverse activities as archery, badminton, basketball, billiards, cricket, dancing, football, golf, rounders, skittles, swimming and table tennis, and we might reasonably expect to find some, if not all, of these as part of the physical education programme of special schools for the physically handicapped. It must be recognised, however, that in these schools we may find a considerable range of disabilities, from congenital handicaps such as cerebral palsy and spina bifida to non-congenital handicaps resulting from traumas, for example road-traffic accidents, post-polio, infantile rheumatoid arthritis, and consequently a wide range of motor ability. Teaching techniques, therefore, may have to be individually tailored to fulfil the main aims of physical education for the children. In general these may be seen as the aims of physical education for the normal child plus the replacement, in many cases, and reinforcement of the developmental play situations experienced by normal children. In some instances we may also wish to teach safety techniques and generally instil personal confidence and esteem.

In an earlier paragraph reference was made to the wide range of activities open to the physically handicapped, and as in the normal school we may expect a progression to these skills from the basic movement training now common in the primary school (balancing, ball catching and throwing, hitting, etc.) to the sophisticated skills. It must not be thought that the activities so far mentioned constitute a definitive list by any means, for stories of legless sub-aqua divers and one-legged water skiers are adding to an ever-growing list of activities open to determined young people and reflect the imagination of dedicated and inspired teachers and advisers.

At many special schools for the physically handicapped the teacher of physical education may often find that the scope of the activities offered is enlarged by the assistance and support of physiotherapists, and a good understanding of the part each plays in the education and life of the children must be established. It will be necessary, therefore, for teachers to read and understand the medical records, for it is assumed that they will have a thorough awareness of the problems that they are likely to encounter. By the same token it is vital that prospective teachers of physical education in a special school for the physically handicapped have some prior opportunity of seeing the children they are going to teach, and have an opportunity of deciding whether they can cope emotionally with what may be a severe deformity. This is particularly important in the swimming pool, where a degree of physical contact may be necessary.

While talking of swimming it is worth mentioning that this is one activity which provides a degree of movement impossible under the constriction of wheelchairs and appliances. Those interested in this area of work will find the Swimming Teachers' Association booklet

Guidelines . . . for Teaching the Disabled to Swim (Trussell, 1971) a valuable aid.

Just as it is impossible to forecast what physically handicapped people, especially the non-congenitally handicapped, are capable of achieving, so it is possible with certain handicaps to foresee limitations and dangers. This is particularly true with epileptics, who prior to a fit may neither be able to see straight nor to think or act rationally. It is thus incumbent upon the teacher in a school where there is a preponderance of epileptics to take precautions such as the liberal use of mats under and around apparatus and the covering of projections on apparatus. Swimming will have to be closely supervised, as will all activities associated with water, but by and large the physical education curriculum in these schools will more nearly represent the normal than that of the more severely handicapped. In spite of this many epileptic children suffer from the same lack of self-confidence and a gradual progression in the degree of difficulty, so that for the children to experience success is as important as it is to avoid 'stress' situations.

This is a maxim that is naturally true for many handicapped people, including the blind, who need to build up confidence from living and playing in a stable environment. Thus new combinations of apparatus in the gymnasium will need to be carefully explained either verbally, diagrammatically on the hand or by feel. Where verbal directions are given they must be related to the known environment, and the teacher may find it is helpful to the child if he teaches from a rather more static position than we might expect in other circumstances.

This confidence in the use of auditory references may be extended, by the use of a bell in a ball or on an archery target for instance, but in many activities only minor modifications are necessary. The use of lane markers for swimming and running is a good example of such minor adaptations. These are not quite so necessary for the partially sighted, but large, brightly coloured balls, hoops, etc., are all helpful. Neither group will be able to play team games with any great skill, nor to play games like tennis, which involve both small balls and rapidly travelling ones. Athletics, especially running, and swimming will generally be successful. Swimming is encouraged in all blind schools for it needs little modification other than the use of manual guidance in the teaching of strokes, lane ropes and auditory cues for turns.

The other major sensory handicap, deafness, needs little

adaptation of the normal programme of physical education. Visual aids will naturally play an important part in teaching methods and all the children should know and respond immediately to a visual sign of warning of danger. The use of percussion instruments which produce vibrations may be helpful in the teaching of rhythmical activities and dance. The teacher may find that particular attention has to be paid to the teaching of basic motor skills as there may be associated difficulties of balance and co-ordination. The major task, however, is to help the children to minimise the social handicap that arises from the inability to communicate effectively.

In the above paragraph, as in several others, reference has been made to the potential of physical education in helping to establish children's self-confidence and esteem and consequently their social adjustment. This thesis has been propagated with some firm basis, for though research in adaptive physical education has been generally sporadic the area of psycho-sociology has been both popular and fruitful. Studies by Biddulph (1954), Clarke and Green (1963), and Cowell and Ismail (1962), for example, have all indicated that there is a positive relationship between superior motor ability achievement and good personal and social adjustment, while Stott (1966) has pointed to the far greater incidence of motor impairment in delinquent children than in normal children. Thus while improvement in social adjustment levels will be an important objective in the teaching of physical education with the physically handicapped, it will assume major importance with such groups as the maladjusted and delinquent.

The implications for the teacher in the latter two areas are therefore clear, for while the programme of work may be near normal it will, nevertheless, have to be individually tailored and graded so that the children experience success and satisfaction from the learning of new skills and receive the approval, both adult and peer, that this success commands. It seems likely that outdoor activities such as climbing, canoeing, camping and hill-walking which induce self-reliance and self-discipline will be a feature of the programme as will dance for girls and perhaps boys as well. Whatever the programme the teacher will have to face the fact that as there is no one single cause of maladjustment, problems can only be tackled by stable and sympathetic teachers who are prepared to spend a great deal of time in organisation and the study of individual children and their needs.

At appropriate stages it would seem to be highly desirable that maladjusted children should be integrated into lessons in a non-special school, but this should be neither rushed nor continued if not seen to be successful, for Adams (1971) has indicated that social adjustment may sometimes be better achieved by special adapted classes rather than an ordinary physical education class. Similarly where 'normal' lessons are adapted, i.e. where all the children are handicapped, significant improvements in motor performance may be achieved with as few as six individual lessons (Keogh and Oliver, 1968). This type of specialised tuition will be particularly valuable to children who are slow learning, have difficulty in conceptualising and perhaps also a language deficit, for example the educationally subnormal. In practice, however, it may be very difficult to provide this sort of opportunity, and the physical education curriculum in an ESN special school will usually consist of those basic activities which would seem to best produce the all-round objectives that are desirable, i.e. dance, swimming, games skill training, and general movement education (gymnastics). Additionally some teachers may favour an approach which places the emphasis on the establishment of personal, physical and emotional security through bodily experiences of different kinds (Sherborne, 1974). It is probable that a combination of the two approaches is the most satisfactory, especially if the latter forms an introduction to the more formal. This is precisely the type of programme that could be advocated for autistic children (Cooper, 1974).

It must not be forgotten when considering the above that the establishment and maintenance of organic fitness is just as important for the handicapped as it is for ordinary people, and it is disappointing that few of the writers in the area of adaptive physical education stress this particular objective. This may be, perhaps, because the mind/body concept is so hackneyed that people pay only lip-service to what they consider to be an ideal. Nevertheless, Oliver (1958) has clearly demonstrated how ESN boys performed significantly better in IQ tests after a period of fitness training, and Morgan (1969), amongst others, has indicated that a relationship exists between physical work capacity and the degree of psychopathology of patients in hospital.

These studies as well as the others mentioned elsewhere obviously have implications for teachers in normal schools as much as for those in special schools, for special classes in physical education may be very advisable for those children whose fitness has suffered from their inability to engage satisfactorily in the ordinary physical education class. This group will include the obese, retarded, disadvantaged and those suffering from what we now recognise as the 'clumsy syndrome' (Dare and Gordon, 1970). All of them will benefit from learning skills in a vigorous and success-orientated atmosphere, and in the case of the obese it may be possible to establish a basis for regular physical activity.

In many schools, both 'special' and 'normal' physical education is often seen as a minor part of the curriculum, and emphasis is placed upon the learning of those skills which appear to be most useful in enabling the individual to contribute to the community in which he lives. Consequently much of the physical education programme is seen as extracurricular, and this can place such heavy burdens on teachers that they are often reluctant to devote time to special classes. The solution may be in involving those outside the profession, for several experiments in involving the community with the recreational activities of the handicapped have proved to be highly successful from all points of view. It is not expected, moreover, that all teachers of physical education should involve themselves in adapted physical education, for even if the rewards are great they do not occur frequently, and the frustrations of both pupil and teacher are many. All that is required is that we have a profession fully aware of the contribution that physical activity can make to the lives of the handicapped and a few teachers knowledgeable enough to ensure that the contribution is more than a token. With new courses opening in our colleges and a new interest in the care and education of the handicapped we cannot be other than optimistic.

Note

1 Copies of Proceedings from The Physical Education Association, 10 Nottingham Place, London, W1M 4AX.

References

Adams, K. (1971), 'The effects of adapted physical education upon the social adjustment and motor proficiency of educable mentally retarded girls', *Am. Corr. Therap. Jnl*, 25, 64–7.

Biddulph, L. G. (1954), 'Athletic achievement and the personal and social adjustment of high school boys', *Research Quarterly*, 25, 1–7.

Clarke, H. H. and Green, W. H. (1963), 'Relationship between personal-social measures applied to 10 year old boys', *Research*

Quarterly, 34, 288–98.
Cooper, D. F. (1974), *The Handicapped*, 'Aspects of Education', No. 16, University of Hull Institute of Education.
Cowell, C. C. and Ismail, A. H. (1962), 'Relationship between selected social and physical factors', *Research Quarterly*, 33, 40–3.
Dare, M. T. and Gordon, N. (1970), 'Clumsy children: a disorder of perception and motor organisation', *Develop. Med. and Child Neurol.*, 12, 178.
Keogh, J. and Oliver, J. N. (1968), 'A clinical study of physically awkward ESN boys', *Research Quarterly*, 39, 301–7.
Morgan, W. P. (1969), 'Physical fitness and emotional health', *Am. Corr. Therap. Jnl*, 23, 124.
Oliver, J. N. (1958), 'The effect of physical conditioning exercises and activities on the mental characteristics of educationally sub-normal boys', *Brit. Jnl Educ. Psychol.*, 28, 155–65.
Sherborne, V. (1974), 'Movement for retarded and disturbed children', unpublished paper, Redlands College, Bristol.
Stott, D. H. (1966), 'A general test of motor-impairment for children', *Dev. Med. and Child Neurol.*, 8, 523–31.
Trussell, E. C. (1971), *Guidelines for the use of those wishing to sit for the Supplementary Certificate for Teaching the Disabled to Swim*, Swimming Teachers' Association.

Part 5

Materials and sources

22

Materials and sources

B. Jagger

Introduction

A considerable amount of helpful information is available to teachers of physical education and can be obtained through education authorities, government publications, specialist physical education organisations, the Sports Council, Governing bodies, voluntary organisations, industrial firms, etc. Teachers who seek personal advancement, enhancement of lesson material and teaching presentation, will find that the Education Committee Organiser/Inspector is a fund of knowledge and also that the headquarters and governing bodies offer much help. The information given in this chapter can only provide a starting point out of which a healthy co-operative association may well develop.

Audio visual aids

There are many sources from which films, film loops, wall charts, etc., can be obtained but catalogues and information lists are regularly revised, so it is possible to give only general information.

(a) *Booklet on Films*, obtainable from PEA, 10 Nottingham Place, London, W1M 4AX.
(b) *Selected Visual Aids in Physical Education* (booklet published by BAOLPE). Apply to Miss K. S. Davis, Organising Inspector of Physical Education, Scottish Life House, 154 Great Charles Street, Birmingham B3 3HS, price 20p.

(c) Governing bodies of sport.
Many governing bodies have available films or film loops on national event highlights, training or techniques. For further information refer to headquarters of governing body; addresses in *Physical Education Year Book*, PEA. See appendix 2.

(d) Local Education Authorities.
Information about films or film loops available from Inspector of Physical Education or Film Librarian, LEA Offices.

(e) Embassies and Cultural Institutes.
Some embassies provide films on physical education and sport. Enquiries should be directed to embassy.

Wall charts, etc.

Wall charts on techniques and skill developments are issued by many governing bodies of sport.

For further information refer to headquarters of governing body. See appendix 2.

Books, magazines, conference reports, etc.

(a) *Books*

(i) *Bibliography of Books on Physical and Health Education, Sport and Allied Subjects*. Brief information about recent books; published quarterly by PEA, price 65p.

(ii) Specialist books from Department of Education and Science, published by HMSO.

(iii) Specialist books compiled by BAOLPE, published by Methuen Educational Productions.

(iv) Certain publishers have specialised sections in physical education and sports, e.g. G. Bell & Sons, Educational Productions, Faber & Faber, Heinemann, Lepus Books, Henry Kimpton, Stanley Paul, Pelham, Routledge & Kegan Paul, Allen & Unwin, Ward Lock, etc.

(v) Some governing bodies issue their own publications, and the majority have handbooks on organisation, skill development, etc. For information refer to headquarters of particular governing body.

(vi) American books are usually more difficult to obtain but specialist publishers include A. S. Barnes, Holt, Rinehart & Winston, Lea & Febiger, Merrill, Prentice-Hall, W. B. Saunders, etc.

(b) *Magazines*

(i) *British Journal of Physical Education*—published by PEA.

Journal of Human Movement Studies—published by Lepus Books.

Sport and Recreation—published by the Sports Council. For address see appendix 1.

World Sports—published by British Olympic Association. For address see appendix 1.

British Journal of Sports and Medicine. For information apply to Dr Evans Robson, 39 Linkfield Road, Mountsorrel, Loughborough.

(ii) Magazines published by governing bodies of sport. The majority of the governing bodies produce their own specialist magazine or newsletter. For further information apply directly to the headquarters of the governing body.

(iii) International Publications.

*International Journal of Physical Education**

(iv) American Publications.

*Journal of Health, Physical Education and Recreation**
*Physical Educator**
*Scholastic Coach**
*Quest**
(*Information available from PEA)

(c) *Reports*

(i) Schools Council.

Titles obtainable from Evans/Methuen Educational, 11 New Fetter Lane, London EC4.

(ii) Association of Principals of Women's Colleges of Physical Education.

Information and conference reports available from Registrar, Nonington College of Physical Education, Nonington, nr Dover, Kent.

(iii) Association of Teachers in College Departments of Education, Physical Education Section.
Information and conference reports available from Mrs. I. Glaister, Fardon House, Frog Lane, Milton under Wychwood, Oxon.

(iv) PEA.
Various conference reports including *Man and His Movement*, Proceedings of 75th Anniversary Conference.

(d) Bibliography of Articles
Bibliography of Articles on Physical and Health Education, Sport and Allied Subjects. Brief information about recent articles published quarterly by PEA, price 90p.

(e) Publications available from Sports Council and Regional Sports Councils. Technical publications, surveys on facilities and provisions for sport, etc.

Courses and further training

(a) (i) Full or part-time post-certificate/ postgraduate courses, including re-training courses are offered through certain colleges and universities. Apply to Registrar of college or university.

(ii) Specialist postgraduate courses are offered at University of Birmingham and University of Leeds. Apply to Registrar at university.

(iii) Specialist courses for intending teachers and qualified teachers in the art of movement, dance and modern educational dance at the Art of Movement Studio, Woburn Hill, Addlestone, Surrey. Apply to the Secretary.

(iv) Specialist courses in recreation management. Apply to Registrar, Loughborough College of Technology or Registrar, Polytechnic of North London, Prince of Wales Road, London NW5.

(v) Information about general courses in *A List of Higher Degrees in Education* available from ATCDE.

(b) Short Term or Vacation Courses

(i) One-term specialist courses in certain outdoor activities. Apply to Sports Council Headquarters, 70 Brompton Road, London SW3.

(ii) Vacation courses in general activities or specialist activities. Apply to the following:
Sports Council Headquarters or Sports Council regional offices.
Headquarters of governing bodies.
Loughborough Summer School.
BAOLPE Summer School.
North Western Counties Blackpool Easter School.
Millfield School, Street, Somerset.
Youth Hostels Association, St Albans, Herts, etc.
General information about grants and awards for vacation courses available from Local Education Authorities, and for long-term courses in publication *Grants and Awards for Higher Education* and *A Programme of One Year Short Courses*, published annually by the DES.

Equipment

General information about gymnastic, games, sports and personal equipment available in advertisements in:
British Journal of Physical Education
Physical Education Year Book
Bulletin of Physical Education
Sport and Recreation
Specialist magazines of governing bodies.
Also from *Harper's Guide to Sports Trade*, published yearly by Harper Trade Journals, Ltd, South Bank House, Black Prince Road, London SE1.

School career awards

Many governing bodies have awards which can become part of school/club work; information is available from the headquarters of the various governing bodies.
The more popular awards presently existing are:

(i) Amateur Athletic Association Five Star Award. A progressive series of awards from one to five star, based on individual performances in three events, two field and one track or two track and one field.

(ii) Amateur Swimming Association. A comprehensive range of awards from elementary to honours level in swimming, survival, etc., including awards for handicapped youngsters.

(iii) Royal Life Saving Society. A progressive and comprehensive series of awards from elementary to advanced levels.

(iv) Amateur Gymnastic Association. Progressive awards based on Olympic Gymnastics including vaulting, agilities, trampolining, parallel bars, rings, pommel horse and high bar.

School Examinations

Many schools are presently embarked on CSE Mode III examinations in physical education. The Schools Council has recently opened up the possibility of an enquiry into possible syllabus content and form of assessment regarding such examinations.

Associations and councils

(i) *Physical Education Association of Great Britain and Northern Ireland.*

The association is a non-governmental body whose objects are to help specialist teachers of physical education to facilitate the exchange of information, knowledge and thought, and to encourage the formation of branches, societies and committees throughout Great Britain. The association promotes research, encourages publications, organises meetings, provides an information and advisory service, supplies speakers, has a reference library and a book department, together with a Resource Centre. In addition, a bi-monthly magazine—the *British Journal of Physical Education*—is published, an appointments register for members requiring posts is maintained and courses and conferences are arranged.

All enquiries, including those for membership, should be

forwarded, with a stamped addressed return envelope, to the General Secretary, Physical Education Association, 10 Nottingham Place, London W1M 4AX, or telephone 01 486 1301.

(ii) *The Sports Council*

The Sports Council was formally constituted by Royal Charter in 1972. The functions of the Sports Council, the Scottish Sports Council, the Sports Council for Wales and the executive Sports Council for Northern Ireland are broadly similar, namely 'to develop and improve the knowledge and practice of sport and physical recreation in the interests of social welfare and the enjoyment of leisure among the public at large and to encourage the attainment of high standards.'

The Sports Council has the following committees: Facilities Committee 'to consider matters relating to the provision and development of urban and rural facilities for sport and physical recreation'; Sports Development Committee 'relating to the development of sport and physical recreation through statutory and voluntary organisations'; Information Committee 'to disseminate essential information and mount suitable research and documentation projects'; Finance Committee 'to consider overall financial policy'.

The Sports Council, working with the governing bodies, assists in the administration of a vast number of courses; full information about these courses can be obtained from the headquarters of the Sports Council or from regional offices. An information centre is also available at headquarters.

(iii) *British Association of Sport and Medicine*

The British Association of Sport and Medicine organises courses and conferences on fitness, human performance, sports medicine, etc., and publishes the *British Journal of Sports Medicine*. Secretary, Dr Evans Robson, see address under Books, Magazines, Conference Reports, section (b) above.

(iv) *British Society of Sports Psychology*

The British Society of Sports Psychology organises conferences and publishes reports. Secretary, Clive Bond, Carnegie School of P.E., Leeds Polytechnic, Beckett Park, Leeds 6.

(v) *Central Bureau*

The Central Bureau provides advice and assistance for educational visits and exchanges. Address: 44 Baker St, London W1M 2HJ.

Appendix 1 Sports organisations

British Association of Organisers and Lecturers of Physical Education	D. H. Williams, Education Office, Park Road, Hartlepool, Co. Durham
British Colleges Sports Association	R. W. Palmer, 28 Woburn Square, London WC1
British Olympic Association	K. S. Duncan, MBE, 12 Buckingham Street, London WC2
Central Bureau for Educational Visits and Exchanges	J. Platt, 43 Dorset Street, London W1H 3FN
Countryside Commission	1 Cambridge Gate, Regent's Park, London NW1
Dalcroze Society	Mrs Althea Heron, 16 Heathcroft, Hampstead Way, London NW11
Duke of Edinburgh's Award Scheme	Secretary, 2 Old Queen Street, London SW1
English Folk Dance and Song Society	K. F. Goode, Cecil Sharp House, 2 Regent's Park Road, London NW1 7AY
Keep Fit Association	Mrs J. Worrall, Room 313, 26 Park Crescent, London W1M 3PB
Lawn Tennis Foundation	J. Moore, Queen's Club, Baron's Court, London W14
National Association of Boys' Clubs	Secretary, 17 Bedford Square, London WC1
National Association of Youth Clubs	Secretary, 30 Devonshire Street, London W1
National Playing Fields	Lt-Col. R. G. Satterthwaite, 57b Catherine Place, London SW1E 6EY

Outward Bound Trust	Secretary, 72 Great Peter Street, London SW1
Physical Education Association of Great Britain and Northern Ireland	P. Sebastian, 10 Nottingham Place, London W1M 4AX
Royal Academy of Dancing	P. E. Start, 48 Vicarage Crescent, London SW11 3LT
Sports Council—Headquarters	70 Brompton Road, Knightsbridge, London SW3 1EX Tel. 01 589 3411
East Midlands Regional Sports Council Principal Regional Officer—R. Logan	26 Musters Road, West Bridgford, Nottingham NG2 7PL Tel. 0602 861325–6
Eastern Regional Sports Council Principal Regional Officer—L. J. Bridgeman	26–28 Bromham Road, Bedford MK40 2QD Tel. 0234 44281 (3 lines)
Greater London and South East Sports Council Principal Regional Officer—Col. B. R. D. Garside, MC	160 Great Portland Street, London W1N 5TB Tel. 01 580 9092
North West Regional Sports Council Principal Regional Officer—C. Ainsworth	Byrom House, Quay Street, Manchester M3 5FJ Tel. 061 834 0338 and 9573
Northern Ireland Office of the Sports Council Secretary—L. G. Glasgow	49 Malone Road, Belfast BT9 6RZ Tel. Belfast 669519
Northern Sports Council Principal Regional Officer—A. L. Colbeck, MBE	County Court Building, Hallgarth Street, Durham DH1 3PB Tel. 0385 64278–9
Scottish Sports Council Secretary—J. K. Hutchinson, CA	4 Queensferry Street, Edinburgh EH2 4PB Tel. 031 225 5544
South Western Regional Sports Council Principal Regional Officer—J. D. Wheatley	Ashlands House, Ashlands, Crewkerne, Somerset TA18 7LQ Tel. 0460 31 3491
Southern Regional Sports Council Principal Regional Officer—R. M. Humphreys	Watlington House, Watlington Street, Reading, Berkshire, RG1 4RJ Tel. 0734 52342 and 57740

Welsh Sports Council Secretary—H. G. Oakes	National Sports Centre for Wales, Sophia Gardens, Cardiff Tel. 0222 397571
West Midlands Regional Sports Council Principal Regional Officer— J. F. Coghlan, MBE, TD, BA	Crest House, 7 Highfield Road, Edgbaston, Birmingham B15 3EG Tel. 021 454 3808
Yorkshire and Humberside Regional Sports Council Principal Regional Officer— F. L. Templeman, BA	5 St Paul's Street, Leeds LS1 2NQ Tel. 0532 36443–4
Youth Hostels Association	H. B. Livinston, YHA, Trevelyan House, St Albans, Herts.

Appendix 2 Schools' sports organisations

The Association for Archery in Schools	S. E. Crisp, Rangemoor, Lytchett Matravers, Poole, Dorset, BH16 6AJ
The Boys' Schools' Lawn Tennis Association	W. E. Curtis, Hon. Secretary/ Treasurer, 50 Royal Hospital School, Ipswich, Suffolk, IP9 2RT J. R. Coates, Hon. Tournament Secretary, 11 Train Avenue, Beverley High Road, Hull
British Schools' Canoeing Association	J. E. Saunders, Education Department, County Hall, Glenfield, Leicester LE3 8RF Tel. 871313, ext. 455
The British Schools' Judo Association	Brian Saunders, Eastbury, 8 Newlands Park, Seaton, Devon, EX12 2SF Membership Secretary— G. Edmondson, Queen's College, Taunton, Somerset
English Schoolboys' Hockey Association	D. J. Newton, Kennedy's House, Aldenham School, Elstree, Herts, WD6 3AJ Tel. Radlett 4306
The English Schools' Athletic Association	J. Forrester, MBE, 'Dunelm', Houghton Road, Newbottle, Houghton-le-Spring, Co. Durham, DH4 4EF
English Schools' Badminton	L. Wright, 5 Starnthwaite,

Association	Crosthwaite, nr Kendal, Westmorland
The English Schools' Basket Ball Association	J. R. Angus, 27 Hillside, Findern, nr Derby
The English Schools' Cricket Association	C. R. Hansford, 11 Coombe Rise, Findon Valley, Worthing, Sussex, BN14 0ED
English Schools' Cycling Association	G. Greenfield, 157 Kingsclere Avenue, Weston, Southampton, SO2 9JR
The English Schools' Football Association	Glyn Evans, 4A Eastgate Street, Stafford, Staffs Tel. Stafford 51142
The English Schools' Gymnastics Association	D. R. Garner, 17 Meadway, Harrold, Beds.
English Schools' Netball Association	Mrs M. S. Thomson, 41 View Drive, Dudley, Worcs., DY2 7TD
English Schools' Rugby League	R. Morgan, 'La Tintelee', Low Moresby, Whitehaven, Cumberland
The English Schools' Swimming Association	E. H. Burden, 190 Nether Street, West Finchley, London N3 1PE Tel. 01 346 6338
The English Schools' Table Tennis Association	D. A. Lomas, 45 Shirley Way, Croydon, Surrey
English Schools' Trampoline Association	L. M. Simmons, 26 Silversea Drive, Westcliff-on-Sea, Essex
The English Schools' Volleyball Association	John Close, 66 Field Avenue, Baddeley Green, Stoke-on-Trent, Staffs Tel. 0782 55958
The Girls' Schools' Lawn Tennis Association	Miss M. E. Parker, 'Cobblers', East Shalford Lane, Guildford, Surrey Tel. Guildford 62122
London Schools' Archery Association	John Summers, Oakfield School Sports Centre, Fencepiece Road, Barkingside, Redbridge
The National Council for Schools' Sports	E. H. Burdon, BSc, 190 Nether Street, London N3 1PE
National Schools' Sailing Association	Harry Cross, Education Department, County Hall, Chichester, Sussex

Rugby Football Schools' Union	R. R. Tennick, Rugby Football Union, Twickenham, Middlesex
Schools' Amateur Boxing Association	W. H. Young, 16 Curtis Road, Hounslow, Middx, TW4 5PT Tel. 01 894 5856

For complete list refer to appendix in PEA Year Book

Index